T0270091

CUSTOMER
360

CUSTOMER
360

MARTIN KIHN

ANDREA CHEN LIN

CUSTOMER 360

HOW
DATA, AI,
AND TRUST
CHANGE EVERYTHING

WILEY

Published by John Wiley & Sons, Inc., Hoboken, New Jersey.
Published simultaneously in Canada.

For general information on our other products and services or for technical support, please contact our Customer Care Department within the United States at (800) 762-2974, outside the United States at (317) 572-3993 or fax (317) 572-4002.

Wiley also publishes its books in a variety of electronic formats. Some content that appears in print may not be available in electronic formats. For more information about Wiley products, visit our web site at www.wiley.com.

Library of Congress Cataloging-in-Publication Data Is Available:

ISBN 9781394273614 (Cloth)
ISBN 9781394273621 (ePub)
ISBN 9781394273638 (ePDF)
ISBN 9781394308668 (oBook)

Cover Design: Wiley
Cover Images: © Alex Mit/Adobe Stock, © Arcady/Adobe Stock

SKY10085551_092024

Contents

Contents

"There is only one boss. The customer."

—Walt Disney

Preface

Every company wants to deliver a great experience to its customers, but very few can do it.

Why not? The challenge isn't really fair: customers' expectations are set by their very best memories—at an Apple Store, with Tesla customer care, Amazon returns, Disney's Magic Kingdom. How can the rest of us compete at that level, with our own (likely limited) budgets and our own (probably understaffed) teams?

The good news is that it's possible to deliver a great end-to-end experience even if you don't have supernatural resources or other special advantages. A new generation of technology is making it possible for almost any enterprise to deliver excellent experiences that truly make sense from end to end—from the moment of awareness through loyalty, service, in-store, on websites, apps, and kiosks, and targeted advertising.

New platforms for data management combined with increasingly powerful artificial intelligence (AI) tools, delivered with respect, create a once-in-a-generation opportunity to break through the competitive pack and win, no matter what your size, industry, or competitive reality.

These platforms are open, heterogeneous, and flexible, and they are even getting easier to use. They are not about signing on to a single vendor for life or buying into a small cabal of power players, like locking yourself into a timeshare you don't really need. Rather, the new winning approach centers on a disciplined delivery of a set of core capabilities.

What are these core capabilities? At the most basic level, there are three:

- **Data:** Organizations have an average of 450 different applications and dozens of sources of customer data. Combining and organizing all this data is a critical first step to delivering a coherent customer experience—and, crucially, to delivering on the growing promise of (you saw this one coming) . . .

- **AI:** AI's potential is virtually unlimited to unlock personalization and insights at the speed of thought, but real risks abound: toxic and unhelpful content, data leakage and insecurity, hallucinations and half-truths, and a lack of grounding to make the output actually useful to your business. Successful, enterprise-ready AI requires a careful approach and the right internal processes.
- **Trust:** Customers and governments alike—not to mention your own, increasingly nervous legal team—require the security, availability, and privacy of data to be locked down. More and more, companies will be differentiated based on their ability to deliver consistently on the promise of trust.

So that's it: Data + AI + Trust. Easy, right? Well, not exactly. But we're all on a journey, and nobody—not even the gold standard enterprises in your industry—do everything right, all the time. As Martin Luther King, Jr., said, "Setting goals is the first step in turning the invisible into the visible, . . . taking the first step even when you don't see the whole staircase."

The goal we've set for this book is to help you take those first steps toward your own Customer 360. We'll show you how the combination of Data + AI + Trust can catapult any company into the next dimension of growth.

***

Introduction

Known for its meticulous Italian craftsmanship, imaginative design and attention to detail, Gucci is one of the most influential luxury brands in the world. Founded in 1921, it is currently redefining luxury for a new generation of customers, building experiences that extend from its retail outlets to its websites and apps and its global client service network, called Gucci 9—a reference to the historic Gucci headquarters campus in Florence.

One of Gucci's goals was to enable its 600 client advisors across seven global hubs to communicate in a clear brand voice, elevating the service experience beyond the realm of daily conversation.

It wasn't easy. Customers engage on multiple channels—inbound calls coming from the website and from stores, WhatsApp, live chat, etc.—and on a wide range of topics, from learning about upcoming collections to making reservations at a Michelin-star Gucci Osteria. To meet the challenge and maintain consistency, Gucci was able to use organized internal data about products as well as previous examples of Gucci communications in its authentic brand voice.

The latter was applied to AI models, which were trained to recommend replies provided to customer care reps. The magic of these AI-generated replies, grounded in product and brand data, was that they were in a "Guccified" tone of voice. The advisors could adapt them for the human touch, but they provided a conversation framework that amplified the interaction—elevating advisors above traditional templates and providing customers with an experience entirely consistent with what they'd expect from the brand.

Gucci is known for infusing beauty into everything it does, including its unique customer experiences. New technologies such as AI help the fashion house practice its mantra, "the human touch, powered by technology," by scaling the capabilities of its advisors with brand-ready messages. As we've said, all companies want to deliver superior experiences from end-to-end to their customers. We all want the Gucci 360, tailored to our own situation. We know as consumers that the brands we feel good about are more likely to get more of our business. It's simple logic.

In one comprehensive survey of 14,300 consumers around the globe, 80% of respondents said that the experience a company provides is as important as their products or services. Take a moment to think about that. Most companies might reasonably assume their customer satisfaction is tied to the quality and price (or the value) of the items and services they sell. But consumers themselves see things differently: they value their *interactions* with companies just as much.

Moreover, consumers increasingly expect a level of relevance or personalization from companies they trust with their data and consent. The same global survey revealed that 65% of consumers expect companies to adapt the experiences they provide to customers' changing needs. In other words, we expect companies to know when we're complaining or just want to get a price quote or the hours the store is open, or when we're in the market for a deal.

Yet the evidence shows most companies fall far short of the ideal. In fact, 61% of consumers said that they felt like the average company treated them "like a number." Forget Guccified or Customer 360, these consumers are saying, just treat me like I'm a human being.

Among business-to-business (B2B) buyers, the situation isn't any better. According to a recent study, 63% of B2B buyers said their customer experience was worse than it could be, and almost as many said that their sales reps didn't really try to understand their needs. These customers, often making big-ticket decisions that can have career-affecting consequences, too often feel like their reps treat them transactionally when what they want is an advisor they can trust.

And there's evidence that as consumer expectations continue to rise, we're getting more demanding—and that companies are falling even further behind. Every few years, dating back to the early 2000s, the W. P. Carey School of Business at the University of Arizona has collaborated on a survey of 1,000 Americans on the topic of customer service. It's a fascinating study that puts a dollar estimate on revenue at risk due to poor complaint handling, among other things.

The study paints an alarming picture of the state of consumer-company interactions. According to the researchers, nearly three-quarters of respondents reported a product or service problem in the past year—more than *double* the level in earlier years. More than half said the problem wasted their time and one-third said they suffered "emotional distress."[1]

And they weren't keeping it to themselves, either: one-third posted negative information about their problems on social media, more than *double* the rate in 2020. In the end, the researchers estimated that about $887 billion of future revenue was put at risk due to poor service, also almost double the amount estimated in 2020. Put simply: people are getting angrier, are sharing their feelings, and are taking revenge where it hurts the most, with their wallets.

Granted that service is just one part of the Customer 360, the study is directionally concerning: either service levels are going down, people are expecting more, or both. Either way, only one of those levers can be pulled by the companies themselves: they need to improve customer experience. Real revenue is at risk in disappointing the people who keep us in business.

> "It's not what happens to you but how you react that matters."
> —*Epictetus*

***

So consumer attitudes and behaviors are changing, as they always have and will. (We'll cover more about consumer trends in Chapter 5.) But they're only one part of the story. There's also the incredibly important role of technology—how it's changing, transforming businesses and work, and upending our assumptions about what it takes to deliver a Customer 360.

"Customer 360": What is Customer 360? We'll be using this term often, and so we want to describe what it means. It's not a particular technology, vendor, or established term of art. *Customer 360* describes a constellation of technologies, processes, and people that are all directed at building a coherent, end-to-end customer experience. It encompasses Data + AI + Trust. The purpose of *Customer 360* is to serve the total customer journey from the customers' point of view, regardless of internal departments, siloes, structures, or habits. So building a Customer 360 just means building a customer experience that makes sense.

We are all adapting to a changing technosphere. Most obviously, the generative AI revolution took most of us by surprise in November 2022, when OpenAI's ChatGPT began to talk to us in ways that seemed quite human, and image-generation tools like MidJourney and DALL-E blew our collective visual synapses.

As we slowly emerged from the economic shock of the pandemic, among other challenges, we faced a technology environment of careful budgeting, some vendor consolidation, reprioritization, and the need to improve our skills. Meanwhile, the pace at which new technologies infiltrate our lives is breathtaking. (See Figure 0.1.)

Believe it or not, it took mobile technologies 16 years to reach 100 million users. (That may be why "The Year of Mobile" kept happening again and again.) It took social networks like Facebook and Instagram only 2.5 years to reach the same milestone, and TikTok just 9 months. Yet ChatGPT reached 100 million users in *two months*, ushering in the era of widespread generative AI (GenAI).

The AI opportunity itself is clear, even if we're not always sure how to proceed. One survey showed that 84% of business leaders agreed that GenAI would improve customer service (good news for the researchers at Arizona State), and two-thirds are hiring people to work in this area. The consulting firm McKinsey is sanguine about AI, forecasting that it will free up 30% of employee time by 2030, generate $4.4 trillion in annual GDP impact, and that three-quarters of companies will be using GenAI in some form by 2027.

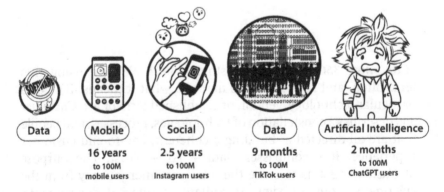

Data	Mobile	Social	Data	Artificial Intelligence
	16 years to 100M mobile users	2.5 years to 100M Instagram users	9 months to 100M TikTok users	2 months to 100M ChatGPT users

FIGURE 0.1 Time to 100 Million Users

FIGURE 0.2 The Three Layers of AI Experience

Most of the companies we talk to seem to believe that their businesses can grow by becoming more connected to customers through the medium of AI and GenAI. At the same time, they believe (hope?) they can use AI to reduce costs, increase employee and process productivity, improve efficiency, and exceed customer expectations. Suddenly, every business transformation is an AI transformation, and companies know they need an AI strategy to be competitive in the near future.

None of the fundamental trends treated by AI and GenAI is new. What the new generation of AI tools and techniques has done is accelerate all timelines, teleport all transformations. We've been on the productivity journey for some time, enabled by technology. Workflow automation has improved, and infrastructure like storage, compute, and bandwidth only gets better. AI now means we can make almost every function more productive, in ways we haven't seen before.

When employees are more productive, businesses can grow faster, with better margins. It's an attractive equation and explains why AI is now the number one priority for business leaders. But in building our Customer 360, how are we to think about AI? What is its role in our formula of Data + AI + Trust?

Let's think about the consumer experience of AI first. We'd argue that this experience has three discrete layers; see Figure 0.2.

- *User interface (UI):* This is the place where the consumer directly interacts with the technology, the thing they log into or the website they visit. In the case of ChatGPT, it was an app that accepted prompts in natural language and would deliver a desired output, like an email, answer, summary, or computer code.

- *Model:* This is the trained model itself, which transforms the input (such as a prompt) into the output (the response). These can be open source and freely available, like Meta's Llama, or more closed, like OpenAI's models.
- *Data:* The foundational level, this is all the data that were used to train the model. In the case of ChatGPT, we assume it was trained on pretty much the entire open web, including Wikipedia, Reddit, podcasts, news reports, etc.

You can see how these levels map to our overall Customer 360 framework of Data + AI + Trust—*except where is the Trust?* That's not a trivial question.

When translating consumer-facing AI like ChatGPT into a corporate setting, the rules change. As fun and exciting as ChatGPT and its relatives are to us as people at leisure, when we become part of an enterprise—delivering a product or service, perhaps regulated, at least constrained by customer expectations and serious business requirements—we have to be *much* more careful. The fact is, consumer-facing AI apps like ChatGPT can't safely and reliably be plugged into the enterprise context without a lot of care.

That's why 88% of IT leaders say they feel they can't meet their company's demands for AI safely—with an emphasis on *safely*. To use AI and GenAI safely, the enterprise needs guardrails around the output; it needs to be sure that what it's automating and putting in front of customers is free of toxicity, bias, hallucinations, and text and images that aren't in the brand's voice.

Specifically, in bringing advanced AI into the enterprise, companies must see to the following:

- Ensure trust and safety: Avoid hallucinations, bias, and misinformation.
- Access the full set of customer data: Free data trapped in different apps, warehouses, lakes, and more.
- Fine-tune AI models using their own data: Make the model relevant.
- Integrate AI outputs into employees' workflows.

All these challenges are real, but when facing AI as a business imperative, the most difficult to solve is the requirement for trust and safety. The fact is, what we could call a fundamental trust and results gap remains with AI. More than half of consumers don't believe AI is secure. Meanwhile, 60% of customer experience leaders say they don't know how to get value out of AI. On both sides—consumers and companies—there's some understandable hesitation in the face of these new powers.

Going back to our consumer AI framework, in the context of the enterprise, the following need to be solved:

- *UI:* A conversational interface for employees such as call-center agents, marketers, chatbots, and more
- *Model:* A way to use powerful open-source and third-party models but also retrain or adapt them using first-party data, to make them your own
- *Data:* Speaking of first-party data, making sure it's secure, gathered with consent, compliant, and used with trust

What's the right approach? It makes sense to start at the foundational level, with *data*. It's been reported that about 71% of the average company's applications are disconnected. Many hard-working enterprise IT departments and others are dealing with hundreds of independent databases, each of which is an island of trapped data. These data sit in mainframes, in apps on the internet, cloud databases, personal computers, and so on.

Moreover, these data are in many different formats: customer relationship management, transactional, unstructured text and images, email, social posts, etc. The volume is undeniable and growing. Trapped data about customers lead directly to a disconnected experience, as each channel works off its own partial view.

Starting 5 or so years ago, a new class of enterprise technology, called the customer data platform (CDP), emerged to solve the trapped data problem. We won't dwell on it here, since it was the topic of a previous book, *Customer Data Platforms* (Wiley, 2020), by Martin Kihn and Chris O'Hara. CDPs continue to mature and provide a more and more flexible solution to the trapped data challenge.

The purpose of the CDP is to build unified profiles of customers and accounts and to make them available to line-of-business users and data specialists. It does this by providing a suite of tools to ingest (or access, in some manner) customer data; harmonize it so it's interoperable; perform identity management; provide or enable analytics; and allow audiences to be delivered to business systems such as marketing, service, and sales.

Now let's take a moment to imagine what a broader solution would look like—one that incorporates a CDP for data management, but also integrates a method to train trusted models on the data in the CDP (and elsewhere), as well as a user interface that fits into the flow of work.

The design principles for a system for Customer 360 in the enterprise might look something like this:

- Integration across all the apps you use for different customer-facing functions—sales, service, marketing, commerce, etc.
- Use of a metadata framework. (Metadata is data about data, or a data taxonomy, that helps different applications work together by ensuring they all speak the same language.)
- CDP as the single source of truth for customer data, with unified profiles for customers and accounts.
- Real-time data collected from the web, apps, and other customer touchpoints, streaming into the unified profiles in the CDP.
- Intelligence in the flow of work—meaning predictive and generative AI and machine learning (ML) are available within the tools used in each department.
- Automation for common tasks and flows, again across departments and apps.
- No-code and low-code model-building tools, so users don't necessarily need to be power players or code adepts to be able to get real benefits.
- Ecosystem of partners, custom apps, learning resources, and talent to make the platform work with other vendors' products and within a sphere of influence with network effects.
- Easy ways to activate decisions and segments on the most common external platforms such as Amazon, Meta, Alphabet; and to integrate the data layer with leading cloud data platforms like Snowflake and Databricks.

These principles adhere no matter what vendors you're using or your industry. A number of leading technology companies are rolling out a platform along the previous lines—one of them, Salesforce, employs both your authors—and a solution can be implemented in numerous ways, including homegrown or hybrid models. What's important is to keep the end in mind.

"Begin with the end in mind."
— *Stephen Covey,* The 7 Habits of Highly Effective People

The current AI revolution will improve productivity. As we've said, McKinsey estimates that 30% of employee time would be freed up by 2030, and 66% of that would be felt in the front office. It will lead to better margins, with a significant impact on global GDP.

And—most important from our Customer 360 perspective—it will lead to better customer relationships. In fact, 84% of enterprise leaders polled by Salesforce recently agreed that GenAI would allow them to serve their customers better. (See Figure 0.3.)

Remember that we're hardly in the end zone with AI; we're closer to the kickoff. As a class of technologies, AI is coming at us in waves:

- *Wave 1:* Predictive—ML models, for the most part, used for years to perform tasks like recommend products or make credit decisions.
- *Wave 2:* Generative—Models that can provide structured insights, summaries, briefings, and imagery.
- *Wave 3:* Autonomous and agents—Relatively self-contained agents that can talk to one another and perform tasks in the digital realm.
- *Wave 4:* Artificial general intelligence (AGI)—A future state when AI can do many of the value-added tasks that people do, just faster.

As we're enjoying Wave 2, we can see that AI in the enterprise is already being incorporated into the flow of work in many different departments, making them more efficient and effective and (we hope) less stressful. The ultimate goal is to put AI to work where it has the most positive impact.

AI is already having an impact in many areas:

- *Sales:* Automating prospecting emails, call summaries, sales summaries, call exploration
- *Service:* Delivering proactive service with automated replies, summaries, knowledge articles, search answers, mobile work briefings
- *Marketing:* Personalizing engagement with bespoke email creation, segment generation
- *Commerce:* Increasing conversion rates with product descriptions, smart promotions, commerce concierge
- *IT:* Developing faster with natural language to code, auto-completion, chat-based coding assistants

FIGURE 0.3 The Four Waves of AI

Ultimately, the nature and tenor of work will change; it is already changing. We will rely on our AI sidekicks more and realize it less. In a way, tools are becoming easier to use even as we ourselves use less of them, relegating much of our more tedious, routinized work to the software, which is able to take on more intelligent tasks, even those requiring a decision. (See Figure 0.4.)

***

Let's return to our original formula: **Data + AI + Trust.**

We've hinted that our answer to the Data term is basically a CDP. This is true, but with some qualifications. Since the release of *Customer Data Platforms*, the CDP market has matured. Originally a tool for marketers—particularly retailers, with complex online and offline data sources and prolific customer communications—the CDP is now used by every customer-focused department, including customer service, sales, IT, finance, and even research and development.

Take London's Heathrow Airport. This major international hub serves 200+ destinations, operates 1,000+ flights a day, and welcomes 79 million+ passengers a year. Operating with the support of around 75,000 people, Heathrow is now Europe's busiest and the world's most frequently connected airport.

"How customers engage with airport services has completely changed," said Meenal Varsani, head of Marketing and Customer Engagement. "Around 90% of passengers now use websites and apps

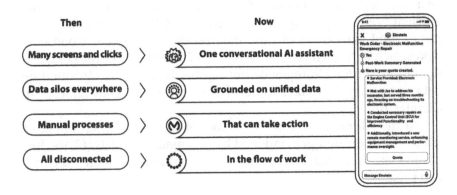

FIGURE 0.4   Customer 360 Changes How We Work

as part of their overall journey." With 14 websites and 45 backend systems, Heathrow Airport was struggling to keep pace with this shift in behavior. "Our digital services were very disjointed," said Bob Stickland, head of Technology for Commercial and Digital Platforms at Heathrow. "We needed to focus more on the customer experience and less on our internal processes."

With the help of Salesforce, shopping, parking, support services, and customer communications now all run on the same platform, which means passengers get the seamless experience they expect. Now, a daughter can contact customer service to check airport security rules for her mom's favorite Penderyn Welsh Cream Liqueur and place an advance order online to collect later at the terminal.

By connecting customer service, marketing, and e-commerce interactions in Data Cloud, Heathrow will be able to anticipate what passengers need before their next visit to the airport. For example, it could see that a business traveler always buys the same products in duty free and reminds that traveler to place a click and collect order.

Heathrow also transformed how it processes online quotes and purchases for its parking services, which has helped to increase conversion rates. "Within a month of migrating our parking services to [a unified platform], we achieved our highest-ever revenue and online Net Promoter Score," said Peter Burns, marketing and digital director.

As our Heathrow example indicates, in addition to expanding beyond marketing, the CDP has become more interoperable with external systems. This expansion includes added pre-built connectors to common sources and stronger APIs, but it also includes an ability to share and federate data to and from cloud data warehouses in a highly efficient "zero-copy" way. In effect, modern CDPs like the Salesforce Data Cloud and others can use data resident in popular cloud data stores such as Snowflake and Google BigQuery without the complexity and expense of lifting-and-shifting the data, greatly streamlining data operations. (We have more to say on the zero-copy concept in Chapter 10.)

At the AI level, there are a number of ways to take advantage of the power of the new generation of large-language models (LLMs) like Claude and Anthropic, in the enterprise, without sacrificing security and trust:

- *Shared trust:* Providing secure API access to an external LLM with a provision of zero data retention on the part of the LLM

- *Vendor-hosted:* A per-tenant model provisioned and hosted on the platform of a highly-trusted vendor
- *Bring-your-own-model (BYOM):* Building and training your own AI model using a data science tool such as Amazon Sagemaker or Google Vertex, and importing parameters into the CDP or data layer
- *Bring-your-own-LLM (BYOLLM):* Building your own LLMs and running it yourself using platforms such as OpenAI, Amazon Bedrock, or Google Vertex AI

AI should also be incorporated into the tools your teams use. We call this bringing-AI-to-the-tools (versus training models, which is bringing-the-tools-to-AI). This is done using built-in features such as natural-language interfaces (e.g., describe a segment in plain language without writing SQL). This is also done using various Copilots, which are virtual search-and-task modules that are also unlocked with natural language prompts and questions. These Copilots, increasingly common, will only get more proactive, intelligent, and able to automate previously manual processes.

That addresses Data + AI . . . but, again, *what about Trust?* We've already touched on this critical component, realizing it's essential to maintain trust with customers, who are skeptical already. Building Trust into the flow of work is a significant challenge. It requires a number of components, each of which is an engineering (and sometimes ethical and compliance) task of no small magnitude. (See Figure 0.5.)

An enterprise AI Trust layer has the following key components:

- *Audit trail:* An ability to log minute details about users, tasks, output, and data sources, often for compliance reasons
- *Toxicity detection:* Removing toxic content, and an ability to define what "toxic" means in context.
- *Zero retention:* Ensuring that no customer data are retained by third-party models used, nor affect third-party models in an indirect way, e.g., by providing training inputs
- *Data masking:* Cloaking personally identifiable information so it is not compromised.
- *Dynamic grounding:* The ability to use first-party data and other company data to direct and adjust the output of the AI and GenAI process (e.g., by putting communications into the brand's voice)
- *Secure data retrieval:* An ability to access company data at scale, securely, in a format that can be implemented by the process

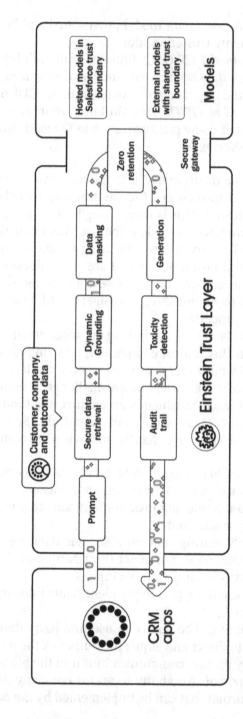

FIGURE 0.5 Trust Layer for AI

In the same way that CDPs revolutionized marketing, a new breed of platforms + AI is breaking down barriers among departments like marketing and service and commerce—and finally giving customers an experience that can start making sense.

Customers around the world expect more all the time, inspired by their best experiences with data-driven brands. Competitive realities require companies to constantly up-level data management, invest in analytics, and rethink the ways they attract, engage, and retain their customers. Economic uncertainties, changing roles for offline channels like stores, sustainability, and relevance imperatives add to an already impressive array of challenges.

New technologies continue to improve our ability to tap into AI, manage customer data more effectively, and integrate CRM. But how can companies—no matter their size or industry—maximize their customer experience technology, ensure they have the right teams and workflows in place, and lay the groundwork to delight customers in the years to come?

The answer is a platform approach based on the pillars of Data + AI + Trust. Mastering these pillars via technology, people, and processes is truly the future of customer engagement.

***

THE FIVE FORCES OF CUSTOMER EXPERIENCE

CHAPTER 1

Formula 1's Race Toward Personalization

People don't usually associate Formula 1 with data or AI. But the "greatest racing spectacle on the planet" has become more like a tech company in recent years than ever before. Formula 1 has transformed into a data-driven customer experience engine, delivering a top-speed Customer 360 to its 700 million fans around the world.

"Greatest racing spectacle on the planet"

—Formula 1 slogan

Formula 1 has seen massive growth in recent years, jump-started by the success of Netflix's 2019 reality series *Drive to Survive*. The show caused US race viewership to triple, attracting new audiences like young people and women. Globally, Formula 1 has 1.5 billion viewers, about 46% of whom can be described as "fans." Yet, less than 1% of them will actually attend a Grand Prix each year.

BUILDING ON ITS GREATEST ASSET

The company's greatest asset is its brand. It represents the highest class of international racing, with open-wheel, single-seat formula racing cars. Its first sanctioned race was in 1950, and since then its portfolio of races, called Grands Prix, have occurred all over the world on closed public roads and international race circuits.

Its cars are among the fastest legal road-course racers anywhere. They have wings front and back, causing a windstorm in their wake.

And they are of course a technical marvel of electronics, aerodynamics, suspension, traction control, launch control, and other aids. It has been estimated that the cost of running a Formula 1 team (including cars, transport, services, and crew) is more than $250 million annually.

A lot of engineering intelligence goes into Formula 1, and over the years it's been the catalyst for a number of technical breakthroughs that had a major impact on performance. These breakthroughs include mid-engine cars, four-wheel drive, aerodynamic "downforce" designs, ground-effect aerodynamics, active suspension, traction control, and turbocharged engines.

In some ways, we can see the company's customer-data race as an extension of its engineering expertise into another realm.

WITHOUT CONNECTED DATA, PERSONALIZATION ISN'T EASY

Multiple data sources make it challenging to understand the F1 fan base.

The thing about Formula 1 fans? They're extremely loyal to their favorite drivers and teams. So, a Lando Norris fan isn't likely to have much interest in a message about a rival team. Personalization at this level was critical for increasing fan engagement—and subsequent revenue.

Formula 1 decided to build out one-to-one experiences for fans at scale. That meant personalizing marketing and improving service experiences with data. And the company manages a large number of different data sources, making it hard to fully understand and segment its fanbase. The company needed a shared view of customer data to delight fans and build audience segments that attract new partners.

Faster service is key to delighting Formula 1 enthusiasts.

Formula 1 interacts with thousands of fans over a race weekend. And they're anything but patient if there are delays or F1 TV login issues. They'll reach out to the company's social media channels or the contact center immediately, expecting an ultra-fast fix. Races are emotional events and regaining access can feel like an urgent need.

Formula 1 doubles the size of its agent team at the start of each season, which helped reduce wait times. And the agents wanted a single, account-based database of fan information that could give them a better picture of the person on the other end of the line, including their marketing, commerce, social, and in-person interactions.

Without shared data, demonstrating partnership value is a challenge.

Behind the scenes, Formula 1's commercial team also relies on aggregated fan data to identify new audience segments and pitch potential partnerships. A single view of data supports the value of alliances to prospective sponsors.

When a sponsor signs, it receives multiple Formula 1 assets, from signage to tickets for former driver appearances and private events. Moving these components from the sales pipeline to account management was not complex. Formula 1 needed a way to easily view partner account details by race event, sponsor, and other advanced criteria.

A NEW ERA OF DATA-BASED FAN ENGAGEMENT

Data Cloud identifies new audience segments, driving personalization, and fan engagement.

Formula 1 adopted a platform from Salesforce called Einstein 1 to bring its numerous data sources into a single view. The platform's customer data-focused Data Cloud is in the driver's seat, surfacing and analyzing audience segments like females, who now make up 41% of the company's fan base. With these insights, Formula 1 can personalize customer journeys and build fan segments that attract new, audience-specific partners like American Express and Puma.

Formula 1 can also tailor marketing content like email newsletters and push notifications about fans' favorite drivers, and stated interests. For instance, Red Bull fans may see an article about the sponsored team. Or, if they've already read it, Einstein 1 Marketing will automatically replace it with other relevant content.

Data Cloud also helps Formula 1 determine a subscriber's likelihood to buy merchandise like a t-shirt or other product within a specific price range. Based on the outcome, Einstein will recommend the appropriate ad to display in the newsletter. Tailored ads have increased Formula 1's ad click-through rates and conversion rates.

Data clarity helps Formula 1 sales prove the value of partnerships.

Formula 1's commercial partnerships team is planning to use Einstein 1 Sales—a business-to-business customer relationship management (CRM) platform—to track deals and sponsorships. So in the future, if the team wants to target a new partner with a niche audience, it turns to the CRM and customer operations team for segmented data to support the potential alliance. With clear segmentation from Data Cloud, the commercial team can prove the value of the partnership to drive the sale.

Once a new sponsor joins the Formula 1 family, the analytics solution Tableau will be used to help the team manage the relationship by tracking partner assets they've received. Tableau dashboards will allow for advanced filtering on criteria like partnership date, race event, or individual sponsor.

Going forward, the company will use analytics and data mining tools to help teams make sense of its massive fan data. Unlike companies in other sports or industries, Formula 1 enjoys an exceptionally high opt-in rate or permission to market to its fans. Yet, data from 20 million known fans can be overwhelming to analyze and monetize. The company's goal is to be able to easily identify when and where fans become part of the "Formula 1 universe." For example, the data may reveal someone became a fan through F1 gaming. Formula 1 can then view all the merchandise the fan has purchased and if they've since subscribed to F1 TV.

Self-service and generative AI will meet fans' needs for in-the-moment support.

Einstein 1 Service helps Formula 1 keep pace with fan expectations for faster support. Ultimately, fans will self-serve on a Formula 1 portal to report login and streaming issues on F1 TV. First-contact resolution has reached over 95%, thanks to automated chatbots and refined processes that agents can use to maintain consistency.

Formula 1 also uses additional services from vendors around race weekends to keep up with support surges. Proactive monitoring minimizes potential service disruptions to keep support running smoothly. Additionally, vendors like Salesforce improve support experiences on owned channels like Formula1.com and F1 TV. By natively integrating chats, calls, and emails, agents have a single view of callers, reducing interaction times by as much as 2 minutes.

Now, Formula 1 service professionals have time to work on open cases instead of juggling new inquiries. This has helped the brand serve more fans, even growing customer satisfaction 8% in 2023.

Soon, Formula 1 hopes to fine-tune support experiences with generative AI. Anticipating fans' preferred language and tone of voice will help them feel more relaxed as agents work to find solutions to their issues.

Results: Data make a difference.

With CRM, data, and AI together, Formula 1 has experienced 33% year-over-year fan growth and an 8% year-over-year fan satisfaction increase just under 90%. Formula 1 support has also decreased resolution times by 2 minutes.

As Formula 1's fan base grows to 1 billion by 2027, Data Cloud and Salesforce's suite of sales, service, marketing, and data solutions will help proactively engage fans and delight sponsors at scale.

GETTING TO THE FINISH LINE

We start with the example of Formula 1 not because it's the most complex Customer 360 ever built, but because it's an example of a methodical roll-out of a program that included technology, processes, and people. It was built on clear goals, was measurable, and was grounded in reasonable use cases that spanned key departments handling the customer experience.

Importantly, this was not just a marketing exercise; it was a customer experience journey. It ultimately encompassed all departments, directly touching the customer. Formula 1 took the following steps:

- Identify the problem and set a KPI that measures it.
- Identify the relevant data sources and their quality.
- Create analytical oversight.
- Implement key technologies after the data audit.
- Organize customer data using a CDP.

- Respond in real-time with a tightly coupled real-time interaction management.
- Give all team members access to the same information.

Since transforming its data usage, Formula 1 now has direct engagement with millions of fans and is on its way to growing its known fan base by 43 million by 2027. As we've said, contact interaction times are 2 minutes shorter on average, and first-contact case resolution has climbed to an impressive 95%.

And what about the all-important fan satisfaction score? It has skyrocketed to nearly 90% positive and increasing year-over-year—a win in any race.

CHAPTER 2

How the Customer 360 Approach Provides Value

If you were watching during our Formula 1 360 race, you noticed we mentioned a couple of significant technology investments—in their case, a CDP and an RTIM system. Combined with some other improvements, retraining, professional services, and new hires, the costs of providing a better end-to-end customer experience can be significant. How significant depends on what you have already, where you're going, your timeline, and so on—but there's no denying that a business case is required.

How do you do this? How does something as amorphous as "a better customer experience" translate into dollars and *sense*?

Customer 360 sits in the pistons of industry, right in the heart of your engine. This combination of technologies and services—integrated as a platform—can be described as piping or plumbing; ingesting data locked up in homegrown and various vendor data stores; organizing that data (harmonization, identify management) and enriching it; and making it available for the newest members of your customer-facing teams to analyze and use.

Customer 360 builds a "single view of the customer," which is powerful if not complete. CDPs are not usually bought as a system of record, like the (much) pricier enterprise data warehouse (EDW) or master data management (MDM) systems. (We talk more about the role of various data stores in the enterprise in Chapter 9.) They are a tool designed to be used by customer-facing teams including service centers, sales professionals, loyalty and commerce associates, data analysts, and more.

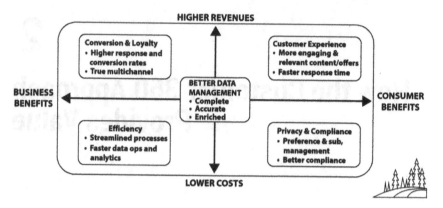

FIGURE 2.1   Customer 360 Value Sources

But while a "single view" is indeed an economic asset, it doesn't have real business value on its own. Little money is made in solitude, at least for technology.

In building out the case for your unified profile of customer **Data** and the related investments in **AI** and **Trust**—and in addressing the question of total cost of ownership (TCO)—we'd like to propose a simple framework.

Its two value axes are (1) Customers and Business and (2) Direct and Indirect, which we've also glossed as Higher Revenues and Lower Costs. Business value is also in (3) data management itself, which is somewhat more abstract.

The framework is shown in Figure 2.1.

1. *Customers and business:* The unified profile is more complete and accessible than any customer profile you already have. (If it weren't, you would use that better profile instead, right?) So the activities you do on the data will be more accurate and insightful.

   In other words, the analytics, reporting, and model building that happens on your customer data will all be better—likely much better—because the basic information they're pointed at is more complete, accurate, and up-to-date. The segments your analysts develop will be more nuanced, accurate, and useful; the predictive models will deliver better predictions; and measurement plans will represent reality more exactly if customer data are carefully combined with outcomes (like sales).

To stick with the Formula 1 analogy, imagine you only had a quartet of Pirelli racing tires, called slicks, medium size, and you were asked to say something about the team using them. Since Pirelli has a monopoly on Formula 1 tires (or *tyres*, as they're called in Formula 1's European markets), you wouldn't be able to say much beyond the generic. You are like the Formula 1 team at the beginning of its Customer 360 transformation, sending the same message to everyone on the list.

Now imagine you had a tail fin and a decal. From them, you might be able to ferret out the make of the vehicle and a sponsor's name, which could lead you to the team. But from this data alone, you wouldn't know anything about recent races or performance, let alone the driver's state of mind. You're like a marketer who knows a person's email and team preference, but nothing about what they're looking to buy or how to engage them.

Economic value accrues gradually, as you collect more and more signals from the customer—*looked at Alpine cars . . . watched a Castrol promo reel . . . checked out the softshell jackets on sale*—enabling you to put messages, offers, images, ideas in front of them that they'd actually want to see. Like that supersweet Fernando Alonso Lights Out 14 T-shirt in teal. *Sold!*

- *Customers:* These can be people, households, or accounts, and they get value from the Customer 360 because their experience is better. More concretely, the images, text, video, and numbers they see are more engaging to them personally, which leads to . . .
- *Business:* The business gains value from the Customer 360 as a result of improvements in the customer experience; higher engagement, done right, leads to greater lifetime value: higher loyalty (or lower attrition), more frequent purchases, and higher basket sizes.

2. *Direct and indirect:* Direct value is easier to measure, things like sales, video completion rates, repeat purchases, basket size. Indirect value includes behind-the-scenes or backstage elements that do have economic equivalents and can be calculated, usually with more effort.
   - *Direct:* Based on your business, direct benefits are the top-line or lifetime value-enhancing benefits.
   - *Indirect:* Workflows and processes are determined by the systems that surround them; people do back- and screen-flips to make things work, often heroically. A Customer 360 allows you to have

more tools to automate away manual steps, increasing productivity and efficiency, which should lower costs or enable the useful redirection of existing resources.

What we're calling direct and indirect benefits can also be seen (as in the previous graphic) as benefits leading to higher revenues or lower costs. Another way to describe this axis is that the top of the y-axis are experiences that lead to a better (more measurably desirable) response; and the bottom of the y-axis are experiences that lead to less (measurable) friction in business processes and in the customer's own relationship with the brand.

Privacy and compliance are called out as a consumer benefit that improves Efficiency/Costs/Friction. The fact is, in many markets, ensuring privacy is a regulatory requirement, and even if it isn't, customer expectations are very clearly on the side of data dignity, respect for preferences, and an ability to control their own data. In a real sense, privacy management lowers legal exposure—a not insignificant consideration.

However, from the consumer's point of view, we'd argue that good privacy and compliance also removes psychological friction. It makes a business easier to work with and instills a level of trust that translates into ease of use. It's often invisible but can express itself in the brand experience. Consumers sense when their data are being used to target them, and they know if they've given permission.

The four quadrants in our diagram fall along these two axes. And right in the middle, most mysterious of all, there is the following:

3. *Data Management:* Most of the value of data management—the purpose of the data layer in our Customer 360, after all—is expressed in the previous regions. But does simply having a more organized repository of customer data provide additional value to the business? We think so.

Students of the science of infonomics recognize data as an asset. It can raise the value of your business, most obviously, if you decide to sell or go public; it also provides option value, giving you an opportunity to do more in the future, if you want. Meaning: the present value of future uses of that data asset already exist in potential. For example, if you decide to launch a new product line extension in the future, you already have a lot of data about customers for similar products.

As everyone with a real skill knows, that skill has no value until used, but its value is always present in unexercised potential, adjusted for risk. We mention this for completeness, although few chief financial officers (CFOs) will grant this argument without a fight. It might help to point them to the now-classic *Infonomics*, by Gartner analyst Doug Laney, which addresses ways to quantify the value of data to an organization. As Laney said: "In supply chain and customer relationship domains, for example, many businesses would rather forego *cash* from business partners in lieu of a *cache* of information."[1]

In the current context, valuing data management has two considerations:

- *Moving from anonymous to known profiles:* As scaled pseudonymous identifiers, such as browser cookies and app IDs disappear, marketing and media all but require first-party data to work. Building a method to collect and organize that (post-cookie) data is a way of buying yourself an option on better ad targeting and measurement now and in the future.
- *Managing technical debt:* Rather than creating an additional data silo, for example, a CDP can unlock information that is trapped within other silos, improving their value. It does this by setting up pipelines, flows, and processes that can transform a legacy data debt (trapped data) into a positive asset (unified profiles).

A reasonable question now is: What is the range of values we can expect to see from Customer 360? What is it worth? Of course, nobody but you can answer this question precisely, in your context. The variables are just too many.

One general guideline we've seen from repeated surveys of customers *after* they have implemented and used a Customer 360 system is that their various response metrics—including response rates to campaigns, engagement rates on websites and apps, and conversion rates for promotions, offers, and general campaigns—improve on average about 33%. This is an aggregate, cross-industry, cross-market benchmark, so your mileage will vary.

That's the average upside. Cost savings seem to average a more modest 15% to 20%, depending on how committed the organization is to hard choices like cutting headcount and contracts. And the monetary benefit of AI varies greatly by context, but it's also definitely positive.

To take an example more or less at random, we recently attended an event hosted by NBC Universal (NBCU) at Rockefeller Center's Studio 8H, where *Saturday Night Live* is filmed. The media company announced the results of a test of generative AI for ad targeting and creative development. Compared to non-AI benchmarks, NBCU saw +21% lift in conversion for a travel company; +29% lift for a casual dining brand; and an impressive +49% improvement in response for a luxury electric vehicle manufacturer.

It's safe to say AI is just beginning to have a measurable impact on every industry. Watch this space closely.

***

CHAPTER 3

Customer 360 in Action: Some Common Tactics

In practice, it is often difficult for those of us involved in a discrete part of the Customer 360, like marketing or service, to imagine specific new tactics. It's not a common habit to think in an end-to-end way about customer experience, despite our best intentions. In this section, we'll present a few thought-starters—ways to envision taking Data + AI + Trust one more step, getting closer to the goal of a holistic adventure.

Remember some of the practical components of Data + AI + Trust:

- Data are available in real time in unified customer (or account) profiles, which access data from multiple internal and external systems.
- Intelligent decisions are made using automation, machine learning, and AI.
- Actions are triggered by "flows" based on user-defined rules or on intelligent decisions.
- Further automation is enabled by ensuring trust in the output.

So data combinations across departments in the enterprise, decisions and flows based on that information, . . . and trust. Some general areas to start brainstorming include the following:

- Cross-selling and upselling
- Personalizing service calls
- Proactive customer service (detecting potential issues)
- Engaging with customers 1:1 at greater scale

- Empowering agents and advisors (with more data)
- Reducing malfunctions and mistakes
- Reframing loyalty for retention
- Improving account-based marketing
- Building privacy-first relationships
- Extracting insights from unstructured data (text, images, audio)

It can be useful to think in terms of *signals* and *actions*—that is, information detected by the platform that would previously have been limited to a siloed system, which in turn can trigger an action or information flow to another system related to the same customer.

Following are examples for a few different industries:

Source	Signal	Action
Financial Services		
Core banking	Customer makes significant deposit.	Create a lead for a wealth advisor.
Website and mobile app	Customer abandons a mortgage application.	Show interest and engagement history in CRM.
Marketing cloud	Customer opens a mortgage marketing email.	Send customer a series of nurturing emails.
Core banking	Customer isn't using new credit card.	Show attrition risk score and next-best action to banker.
Core banking	Customer is nearing final loan installment.	Show auto loan content on website and marketing messages.
CRM	Commercial banking has several CRMs	Create cross-selling opportunities across lines of business.
Retail and Consumer Goods		
Customer care	Customer raised multiple cases in the last week.	Show attribution risk score and recommend next best action to agent.
CRM	Consumer is highly engaged with customer.	Send targeted email to cross-sell.

Source	Signal	Action
D2C commerce	Consumer added an item to cart but did not check out.	Send push notification with an offer.
CRM	Consumer raised multiple cases in the last week.	Escalate case to provide VIP service.
Sales history	Consumer has purchased a new product.	Decrease ads sent to consumer and begin pushing complementary products and enablement.
Healthcare and Life Sciences		
Electronic health record	New patient record created.	Create a new lead allowing providers to offer personalized care.
Clinical trials database	New trial enrolled.	Trigger a notification to the appropriate healthcare provider.
Medical device monitor	Device malfunction detected.	Generate a service ticket alerting technician to address the issue.
Prescription management system	Prescription refill requested.	Automatically update the patient's profile notifying the provider of the refill request.
Health monitoring wearables	Abnormal vital signs detected.	Trigger an alert notifying the provider of the abnormal vital signs.
Electronic medical claims	Claim denied.	Automatically generate a task alerting the staff member to investigate and resolve the claim.
Manufacturing		
Website	New consumer visits customer's website.	Personalized journeys are automatically launched based on preferred channel.

(continued)

(*continued*)

Source	Signal	Action
CRM and third party	Consumer places an unusually large order with a tight deadline.	Predict potential bottlenecks in production line, analyze supply chain data, gain insight into ordering patterns.
CRM and website	Consumer often visits pages related to frequently ordered product.	Predict future customer behavior, improve customer service, and enhance customer loyalty.
CRM and internet of things (IoT)	IoT sensors detect a significant drop in the forklift's hydraulic pressure.	Populate a shopping cart with replacement part and schedule a work order for a service technician.

Among the many use cases for Data + AI + Trust is better coordination of departments such as sales and marketing. A Customer 360 platform strategy can also address the following general requirements:

- We need to find engineering efficiencies.
- We want to increase agent productivity by giving them quicker access to customer data.
- Our sales teams are bogged down by bad data, and it's hurting their productivity.
- Our executives need to see the entire business across multiple organizations.
- We just merged and need to consolidate our software organizations.
- We need to be able to use data across our enterprise to forecast better.
- We need to provide more personalized customer experiences.
- We want to increase efficiency by using AI and automation to improve employee's jobs.
- We want access to all their engagement data to trigger real-time experiences for customers.
- We need to get to a single view of our customers and their data.
- We need intelligent insights to help sales maximize revenue and productivity.
- We need to improve productivity by automating processes across departments.

It is often a good idea to engage outside experts to help manage change. They have the advantage of perspective and experience.

We asked Don Dew, senior director of Salesforce Solutions Consulting at Publicis Sapient, *to provide some on-the-ground examples of clients at various stages of their Customer 360 journey.*

1. *Aligning to the business objective, i.e., "North Star"*

In conversations with a major financial institution, we were told of a common challenge: a lack of availability and trust in the data made available to relationship managers. The inference was that there was a data integration problem.

It should go without saying, but in practice, I've seen a lot of technology projects where the business objective went out the door and teams are robotically processing tickets and building requirements.

The business objective needs to be intentionally defined. We refer to this as the "North Star." It might look like revenue growth, customer retention, employee satisfaction, etc., and be supported by key performance indicators or objectives and key results (OKRs) to get there.

It is important also to realize that the North Star probably has business and technological guardrails. It isn't necessarily a blank slate, and that can be very beneficial to focusing a program.

It is crucial to establish this alignment between the business and technology and to develop a steering committee with the charter of continually adjusting and fine-tuning the focus and metrics of the program on business outcomes.

Through a series of conversations and workshops, it became clear that the real business problem was that relationship managers did not have access to data in a usable format at the right time. This was an experience problem, and the stakes were measurable in both efficiency and effectiveness. This insight enabled alignment to a North Star, and quickly set the stage for how data and AI could create real business value.

2. *Calibrate to where you are today (current state/"as-is")*

Working with a major pharmaceutical company, we uncovered a widespread challenge: their data and capabilities

(continued)

(continued)

were fragmented across different brands and regions. The company expressed a strong desire to centralize resources, empower their teams more effectively, enhance business impact, and harness their diverse data repositories for AI enablement.

It should go without saying, but in order to get somewhere, you need to know where you are.

Current state calibration is bread-and-butter business process analysis, business and technology capabilities mapping, maturity indexing, use-case development, etc. The purpose of the exercise is to calibrate the business to the starting point and prioritization for the program roadmap. It should identify the key use cases needed to build toward the North Star. It also confirms the technical capabilities required to meet the objective.

In the previous example, we interviewed dozens of stakeholders in business and technology to create a capabilities map and overlay it with relative levels of maturity. This process identified some high maturity capabilities that we could leverage for "quick wins" and others that would need to be developed over time.

3. *Building a roadmap for incremental delivery (future state/ "could-be")*

Direct and indirect remuneration (DIR) fees, in essence, are fees paid by pharmacies across a number of performance factors, including patient adherence ("Did the patient take the prescribed medicine?"). Since the inception of this program, retail pharmacy costs have risen so rapidly they threaten the existence of local and regional retail pharmacies. We were approached by one with the basic problem statement of stopping the growth of these fees.

In this step, we fuse what we know about the current state (high fees) with the objectives (stop fee growth) and create a work-back plan. This plan must contain two features:

1. A mapping between business capability with the underlying technology that enables it.
2. A logical sequencing of technology enablement that progresses the capability toward the North Star while delivering measurable value in short increments—and takes into

consideration best practices for design flexibility and modu-larization.

In my experience, this is a very difficult step for people because it introduces the dimension of time—and the longer the time horizon, the more "what-if's" come into play—which causes the "stall."

Managing this requires leadership willing to act without perfect knowledge. The most effective roadmaps look like the "rocks in the jar" analogy. The 18-month horizon starts with the big rocks (knowns) in the jar. The 12-month horizon adds gravel (moderate detail). The 3-month horizon adds the sand (high fidelity). This plan gets iterated every 3 months, with the next horizon's detail being updated to reflect learnings from the prior period's work.

This simple (but not easy) exercise, when fused with the North Star and current state analysis, yielded some incredible findings for our retail pharmacy. The most important was that implementation of the Salesforce Data Cloud could not only feed the Health Cloud and Marketing Cloud, but it could act as a foundation for multiple new programs that could drive new workstreams like data monetization and retail media.

To minimize distraction, we set the near-term focus on foundational use cases that stacked nicely with no rework risk, and we put the North Star opportunity in the background for further evaluation.

—*Don Dew, Publicis Sapient*

***

CHAPTER 4

The Five Forces of Customer 360

So far, we have outlined the components of Data + AI + Trust and made a case for their importance. We described some companies already on the track like Formula 1 and others like Gucci embracing the *dolce vita* of a connected customer experience beyond marketing. We've proposed a valuation framework and specific tactical inroads made by hard-working enterprises who are keeping the finish line—the truly connected customer experience—in their headlights.

In this chapter, we will lay out a new framework for developing your unique Customer 360 approach. Each company is different, but the principles of Data + AI + Trust are omnipresent. How are we to evaluate our market, determine our competitive strategy, and develop a technical and process architecture for the win?

> "In every competition there are no losers and winners, only learners."
>
> —*Brian Herbert*, Dune: House Atreides

THE FIVE FORCES OF COMPETITIVE STRATEGY

"The essence of strategy formulation is coping with competition. Yet it is easy to view competition too narrowly and too pessimistically."[1] So began Michael Porter's article in the *Harvard Business Review* introducing his influential "Five Forces" framework, later elaborated in his instant classic and still best-selling book, *Competitive Strategy*.

At the time of Porter's original essay, strategic frameworks tended to be too academic and detached from the realities of business in the world. Porter opened up the strategic aperture and encouraged business leaders to evaluate the entirety of the environment, from customers to suppliers, inside and outside, inputs and outputs—and even threw in an element of human psychology.

Porter's Five Forces, paraphrased, are as follows:

1. Threat of new entrants: How protected is the business from Factors include barriers to entry, economies of scale, strong existing product differentiation, large capital requirements, regulations, and switching costs.
2. Customer power: How much power does any particular customer have? This is affected by the size of the purchase (e.g., Walmart has a lot of power versus consumer goods providers), number of buyers, switching costs, price sensitivity, and even customer savvy.
3. Threat of substitutes: Is there a similar product or service that does the job? Factors here include the perceived difference between products (brand power), actual differences (product superiority), customer loyalty, and perceived value.
4. Supplier power: How much power do suppliers have? Powerful suppliers can raise costs, limit resources, and their power is affected by their number, importance, uniqueness and ability to do what you do (called forward-integration).
5. Competitive rivalry: How rational is competition in the business? This is the element of psychology, acknowledging that some competitors don't behave like computer programs.

Different industries at different times have varying levels of competition. Porter's examples ranged from fast food (highly competitive) to aircraft manufacturing (less competitive), based on the prevalence of the different forces.

> "If you're entering anything where there's an existing marketplace, against large, entrenched competitors, then your product or service needs to be much better than theirs."
>
> —*Elon Musk*

We reprise these Five Forces not to remind you of your long months back in business school but because (1) Customer 360 is a competitive strategy and (2) the place to start when building out your Customer 360 strategy is to situate yourself in the context of your industry—the competitors, dynamics, rationality, buyers, sellers, etc.

Now we'd like to propose a version of the Five Forces adapted to the question of customer experience. (See Figure 4.1.) Inspired by Porter's forces, the Five Forces of Customer 360 pivot around two axes:

- *The Business*—from the inside out, these are the ways you reach customers and the specifics of your technology stack. Front end leads to back end.
- *The Environment*—from the outside in, considerations are customer expectations and the hard realities of your world (laws, budgets, etc.). Inside (customer) world leads to outside world.

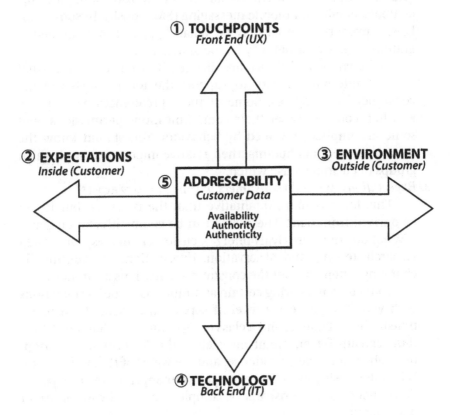

FIGURE 4.1   The Five Forces of Customer Experience

Finally—as we saw in our valuation framework in Chapter 2—the following is right in the middle:

■ *The Data*—as an asset and its limitations, including privacy.

You'll note that our *y*-axis (*Technology* to *Touchpoints*) and our *x*-axis (*Expectations* to *Environment*) can be called the Ts and Es, while the center (*Access*) is *Data* or a "D." So a mnemonic could be TED, where we'd love to present this idea sometime.

We'll go around the axes starting counterclockwise, at the top:

1. *Touchpoints: How do you reach customers, literally?*

    You can communicate with customers through a discrete number of surfaces, and these do change. In a marketing or service context, primary methods may be your website or mobile app, chatbots, email, and mobile messaging (SMS, push). In some markets, a primary channel may be WhatsApp, and in some demographics, a key channel may be social messaging.

    The channels of choice are dictated by what you offer—that is, your internal capacity to support the touchpoint—and the consumers' preferences. Some of these preferences are explicit, as when consumers set their communications permissions, and some are implicit, revealed by behaviors. You should know the most-trafficked touchpoints, their relative importance, and which groups of customers use which.

2. *Expectations: What do consumers in your industry expect?*

    This force is more qualitative than the previous, but it can be derived from data. These data can be competitive intelligence ("What do your best rivals offer?"), customer surveys, syndicated research, testing, and observation. Expectations are continually changing, often without the consumers' conscious awareness.

    Your customers bring certain assumptions to their interactions with you. They expect a level of service, a reasonable response time in the call queue, and a class of reaction from chatbots. When they sign up for an email newsletter, they're bringing assumptions about the quality, cadence, and relevance of that touchpoint. When they visit your website or open your app, they bring expectations about the responsiveness, completeness, and ease-of-use of that channel.

3. *Environment: What are the outside factors that impact your business?*

We live in environments that change all the time. This makes life interesting but forecasting difficult. In general, outside factors affect your competitors as well as yourself, but likely you're in a different position to respond, either better or worse. Obvious examples of environmental factors that affect your Customer 360 strategy are the economy and sentiment, interest rates, inflation, regulatory changes, and political pressures.

Some less obvious but still potent environmental factors include climate change and weather patterns in your markets; the general nature of your competitors (including their rationality, per Porter's Force #5); the borrowing or stock-issuing environment for your company; labor unrest, strikes, and other disruptions in your markets; and the general optimism or pessimism of the times, with respect to consumption.

4. *Technology: What technology is available, and what can you use?*

Technology is the engine of your Customer 360. It's not the entire story, but it's critical. And your Customer 360 technology stack is deep, encompassing all data relevant to customers and their experiences. Your technology picture includes both your existing (legacy) technology stack and contracts, but also a consideration of what is available—what is state-of-the-art—and what you might use in the future.

Another key consideration is your organization's ability to make full use of its tools. Organizations have different levels of expertise at different levels of the stack. Some have a great IT department and well-documented data but less adept product marketers or agencies or perhaps an under-resourced contact center or loyalty team. Technology does not work itself, so a realistic skill assessment is always a strategic filter. (Of course, skills can be improved, just like technology.)

5. *Access: What customer/account data do you have, and how available are they?*

This force is about your data asset. Judged by their growing investment in first-party and zero-party data (the latter are data you request from customers, while the former are any data you collect from them), most global enterprises appreciate its importance. In fact, when asked by McKinsey what their key initiatives

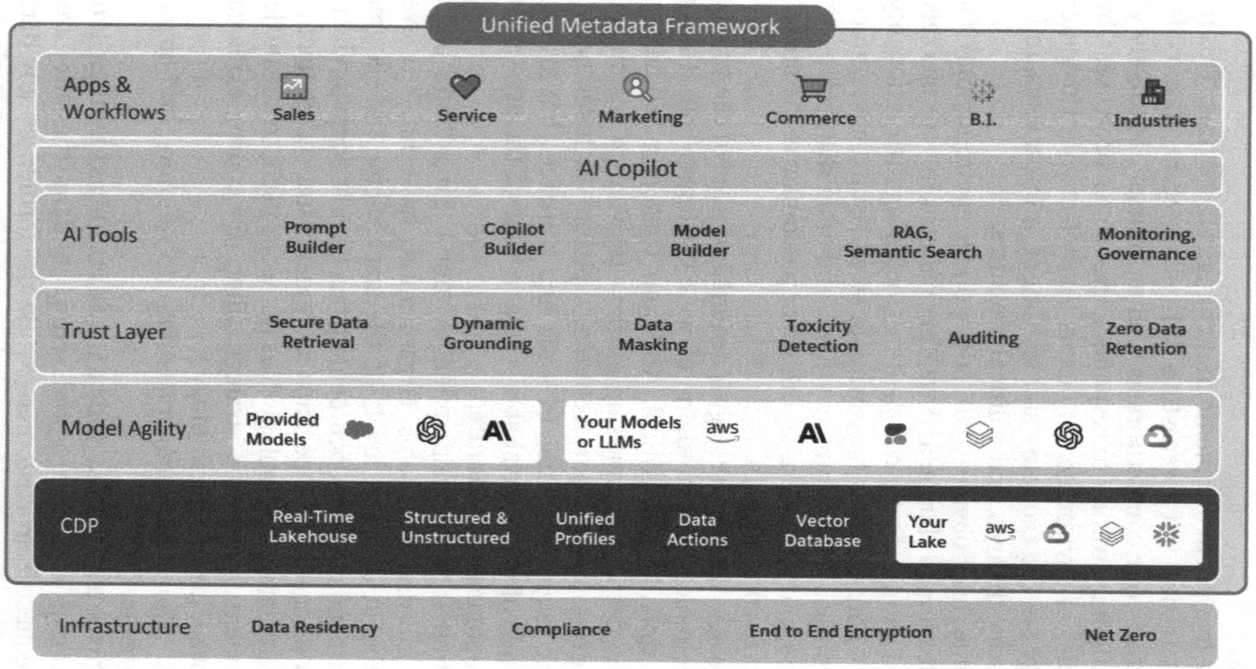

Unified Metadata Framework

Apps & Workflows	Sales	Service	Marketing	Commerce	B.I.	Industries

AI Copilot

AI Tools	Prompt Builder	Copilot Builder	Model Builder	RAG, Semantic Search	Monitoring, Governance

Trust Layer	Secure Data Retrieval	Dynamic Grounding	Data Masking	Toxicity Detection	Auditing	Zero Data Retention

Model Agility	Provided Models	Your Models or LLMs

CDP	Real-Time Lakehouse	Structured & Unstructured	Unified Profiles	Data Actions	Vector Database	Your Lake

Infrastructure	Data Residency	Compliance	End to End Encryption	Net Zero

FIGURE 4.2 Architecture for a Customer 360

would be in the next 12 months, 70% of leaders ranked "Further investment in zero- or first-party data" in the top three.[2]

We all know the importance of customer data in the Customer 360. But not all customer data are created equal: in order to be useful, it must be accessible. A number of subforces can impact access to your own data:

1. *Availability*: What kind of data do you actually have? Is it sufficient? Is it formatted in a way that it can be unlocked (untrapped) from its source?
2. *Authority*: What permission do you have to use the data? Consumers have rights as well as expectations in this domain, and these vary by geography.
3. *Authenticity*: How accurate and timely is your customer data? This may seem like an obvious consideration but is often overlooked. Inaccurate data are actually worse than no data at all, since it skews predictive models applied to other customers.

PUTTING TOGETHER A STRATEGY

The Five Forces of Customer 360 are a guide to determining a path forward. In the following chapters, we'll help you get a handle on the *x*-axis as we take a more data-driven detour into the forces impacting the customer (Chapter 5) and the general business environment (Chapter 6). After that baseline, we spend most of the rest of the book talking about the *y*-axis—the Touchpoints and Technology—and of course the foundational element of Data.

After he'd described his Five Forces, Michael Porter was asked how a company could go about building a strategy using his framework. He recommended the following steps, which we'll paraphrase and adapt to apply to our own Five Forces of Customer 360.

Steps to Develop a Strategy

1. Define the industry. Analyze your own business and its economic, technical, and data-driven dynamics.
2. Identify the key players. Enumerate the major competitors and other entities that impact your business in different markets (including regulators).

3. Assess strategic strengths. Describe your own strengths on the dimensions of customer experience, including brand position, technology stack, and expertise; do the same for key competitors.
4. Evaluate the Five Forces. Go around the clock and try to understand customer expectations, environmental challenges, the weight of touchpoints, and available technology.

Having taken these steps, you're in a good position to begin mapping a Customer 360 strategy that makes sense for your business. Note that Porter was smart enough to include a final step in his strategic framework, one that should keep us all humble.

5. Identify what you can and can't control. And of course, focus on what you can control.

"The competitor to be feared is one who never bothers about you at all, but goes on making his own business better all the time."

—*Henry Ford*

***

CHAPTER 5

What Do Customers Want Right Now?

In this chapter, we'll focus on the *customer* side of the Customer 360—on their behaviors, habits, channels, preferences, and attitudes. To do this, we've sifted through many different data sources, organized by theme. Our goal is not to be encyclopedic but to ground and influence your own thinking about your Customer 360. At the end of the chapter, we'll pull it all together into a list of what we believe are 14 megatrends in customer experience.

WHERE ARE ALL THE CUSTOMERS?

If the average adult consumer's "media day" were a clock, Figure 5.1 shows what it would look like.

The clock varies by age, of course, with younger people spending more time online and less time (tragically) reading. And there's overlap—called multitasking—across channels.

More than 5 billion users are on the internet now, or 65% of the global population. Most of us are highly mobile. More than 90% percent of these internet users access the web on a mobile device at least part of the time. The mobile share of daily internet time continues to grow quickly, from 28% of total time 10 years ago to almost 60% today.

Social media is still a major time sink—uh, locus of connection—but it's extremely focused, due to network effects. Each month, the average time a person spends on YouTube is almost 24 hours (a full day). Facebook is close behind at 20 hours, and WhatsApp

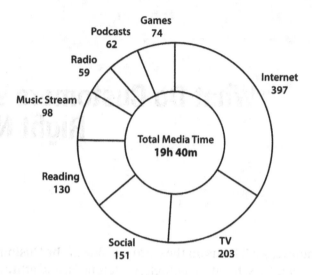

Games 74
Podcasts 62
Radio 59
Internet 397
Music Stream 98
Total Media Time
19h 40m
Reading 130
Social 151
TV 203

FIGURE 5.1   Daily Time Spent on Media (mins.)

consumes more than 17 hours. In fact, you can reach 61% of the American public (over age 13) on Facebook alone. On TikTok, you can reach 43% of adults.

It's always important to keep a global perspective. Believe it or not, the United States is home to only 6.7% of total internet users. East and South Asia (including China and India) together claim 42.5%; add the rest of Asia (including Japan), and you're almost at 60% of the total.

In terms of discovering a brand—a key consideration for marketers—the most important drivers are search engines like Google (31% of internet users report using search engines to find retail products), ads on TV (30%), word of mouth from friends and family (27%), and ads on social media (27%). If you're wondering about influencer marketing, it's now a $20 billion industry, double what it was in 2021, and it leans toward men and Instagram as a channel. About 25% of people admit to following influencers online (and many others are lying).

For the most part, consumers prefer to be contacted using different touchpoints, depending on the context. This is intuitive, and many companies will ask consumers to select preferred channels (email, SMS, mail). Top preferences for adults, according to a recent study, are shown in Figure 5.2.

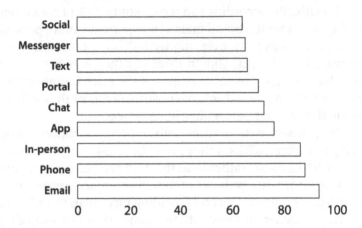

FIGURE 5.2 Preferred Contact Channels (%)

Most customers say they expect to be able to do anything online that they can do in person or over the phone, and the overall share of customer interactions that take place online—versus in person or via phone—was well over half in 2024.

Not surprisingly, younger consumers are more comfortable with digital channels. In fact, they can sometimes seem real-world averse. Fully 65% of millennials said they preferred to engage with companies digitally, while the average for older adults was under 50%.

ATTITUDES TOWARD PERSONALIZED EXPERIENCES

Attitudes toward personalization are difficult to capture accurately. After all, like an excellent waiter at a high-end restaurant who manages to magically appear exactly when you need him, as though he has always been there, personalization done correctly does not feel like targeting. It just feels like good service. The customer doesn't even need to be aware it's happening; they just need to know the experience works.

Most surveys we've seen indicate that consumers in general, in most markets and industries, are open to more relevant experiences based on their first-party data, with consent. There's also evidence for a real business impact due to personalization. Both the expectations and the impact are higher for younger consumers and are higher in certain more mobile-centric regions like Brazil and Hong Kong.

Specifically, according to a recent study, 57% of consumers say they will spend more if a brand makes its experience more personal to them (defined broadly). An even higher 86% say personalized experiences increase their loyalty. One in three say they will buy a product again after having a good experience even if the price is higher than competitors. Conversely, two-thirds of consumers report they will stop using a brand that doesn't personalize in some way.

In terms of data used to deliver personalization, consumers are fairly consistent: 67% say they prefer brands to only use their first-party data, with consent, rather than third- or second-party appends.

Consumers are well aware that most enterprises are trying to capture their first-party data and providing incentives to authenticate or log in. They're generally okay with this (since they're aware of it), but their expectations rise in tandem. They say they expect *better* personalization when they provide more data (74%) and when they spend more (64%).

FRUSTRATIONS AND EXPECTATIONS ABOUT PERSONALIZATION

Unfortunately, at present a gap exists between customer expectations and companies' ability to deliver. One report found that 73% of customers expect companies to understand their unique needs and expectations, but 56% felt that companies treated them generically. This is in line with a different study that found that 53% of customers expect companies to anticipate their needs, while only one in three felt that companies could do this.

One expectation that's consistent across the data is—ironically—about *consistency*. It's clear that most consumers expect a consistent experience from companies but are frustrated by the current state of the art. "Consumers' number one frustration with organizations is disconnected experiences—feeling like they have to start over every time they talk with someone new," said one analyst, whose own research found that 55% of consumers felt they were engaging with entirely separate departments across the enterprise.[1]

Frustration with disconnected and inconsistent experiences is rising across the globe. In the United States, more than half of consumers admitted they were "frustrated" by inconsistent experiences, up from 41% in 2021. There were even more notable pockets of annoyance elsewhere: in France and Italy, for example, around three-quarters expressed frustration.

So disconnection is an issue. Another source of friction is the speed of companies' ability to respond to questions, complaints, and other experience dimensions. Consumers are aware of technology's progress, and their expectations are rising. More than 80% of customers say they "expect" faster service as technology advances. As we've said, they're also apparently aware of data collection. So not surprisingly, 80% say customer experience should be better, considering all the data companies are collecting.

On the positive side, those companies that deliver better, faster, more connected experiences see clear returns. We've seen that good experiences improve reported loyalty and repurchase. Consumers also say pleasant encounters make them spiritually generous: 75% say they'll forgive past mistakes after a positive experience.

EXPECTATIONS AROUND PRIVACY AND CONTROL

Privacy and personalization are tightly coupled. It's not possible to deliver a personal experience without some (first-party) information about a consumer, and yet many consumers say they're reluctant to provide this information, even as they expect the experience. It's a paradox. It even has a name in academic circles: the Paradox of Privacy.

One attitude is almost universal: 98% of consumers say they want brands to do more to guarantee the privacy and security of their data. And when they become uncomfortable, people are more and more likely to do something about it. There has been a 69% increase in user data deletion requests on platforms in the past 2 years.

On the open internet, between 30% and 50% of users (depending on the market) say they're worried about how companies are using their personal data. Globally, the trend is to look for explanations and remain vigilant. (See Figure 5.3.)

The best way to get consumers to feel more comfortable sharing their data is to act responsibly. Be honest and open, jargon- and angle-free. Fully 71% of people say they're more likely to trust a company

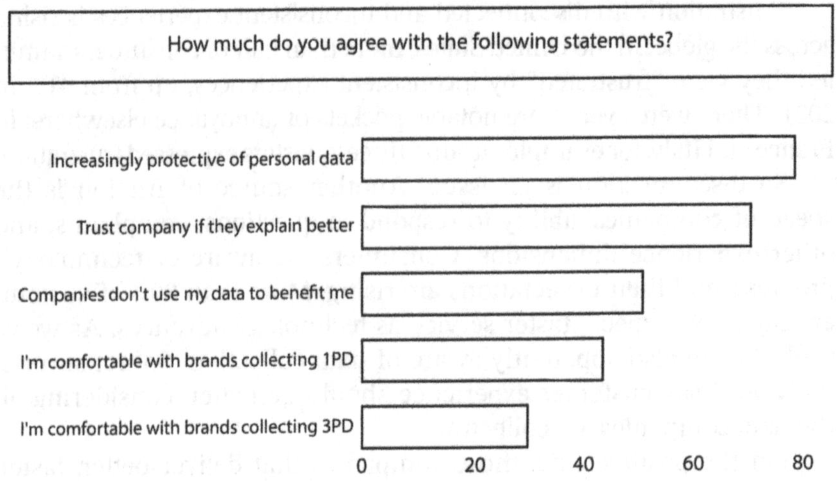

How much do you agree with the following statements?

FIGURE 5.3 Privacy and Trust Preferences (%)

with their data if its use is explained in plain language. And companies must overcome cynicism, as only about one in three people think that their data are used mainly to improve *their* experience (as opposed to serving the company's interests).

Around AI, it's safe to say attitudes are changing monthly, and the relationship of new GenAI models and methods to personal data and privacy is not well defined. Most people still tell surveyors that they think AI will improve their lives. But it's also clear that most consumers (58%) say they're "highly concerned" or "concerned" about the implications of AI on their own data privacy.

Communicating the purpose of data collection and its use is a business requirement and the same is equally true of AI employed in the course of the Customer 360.

***

FOURTEEN MEGATRENDS IN CUSTOMER EXPERIENCE RIGHT NOW[2]

A lot of forces are rocking customer experience these days, and they don't all start with AI. The good news is that enterprises are leaning more on customer experience (CX) as the discipline closest to the customer. Seventy-eight percent of CEOs say they're looking more at CX for growth, according to a recent survey.

The bad news is, in a word, pressure. Pressure for results—and the relentless requirement to stay on top of what's happening with customers, markets, and technology. It's no wonder that chief marketing officer tenure is stuck at its lowest point in 10 years, according to search firm Spencer Stuart.[3]

Based on our conversations with customer experience professionals across the globe and surveys, here are 14 candidates for the biggest trends in Customer 360 today:

1. We're in the age of the post-verbal consumer.

   Consumers are moving their "like" button from text to images to video. Bloggers are trending to video; logos are going text-free. And videos are getting shorter: YouTube reported explosive growth in views of videos under 1 minute. The TikTok Effect is here—what? Squirrel!

   What to do (WTD): Master short-form video or hire someone.

2. Tolerance for any friction is going to zero.

   Ranging from slight delay in page-load time, confusion at the checkout, to disappointing product recommendations, 80% of consumers say they'll drop a brand after three bad at-bats. Money is to be made in removing friction. Look at what Tesla did to the car-buying experience.

   WTD: Look for places to get the lead out.

3. Generational labels no longer work.

   Millennials are self-centered and experiential; baby boomers are smug and judgmental. Like most stereotypes, these aren't very useful. We're splintering along different lines these days, and Pew Research announced it is downplaying generational labels.

   WTD: Pay attention to behavioral drivers (location, mood) instead.

4. Survey responses are getting less reliable.

   Surveys—that aging staple of the insights team—are getting harder to do and less reliable. Response rates are down, and

   (continued)

(continued)

    people online are more performative. Some analysts suggest up to 50% of people give misleading responses.

    WTD: Rely on more in-depth (and offline) surveys.

5. People are more paranoid—especially about data.

    A series of public data storms—Snowden, Cambridge Analytica, leaks—and deep dives like the *New York Times'* "What Do They Know and How Do They Know It?" made consumers wary. Google search trends for "tracking" are up 25 times in the past 20 years, and the United States still doesn't have a federal privacy law.

    WTD: Overshare what you're doing with data—and why.

6. The Paradox of Privacy is real and really important.

    Consumers think and act in weird ways with data. This is the Paradox of Privacy. Eighty percent of consumers say they feel little control, yet 48% will share information. We can't decide whether to opt-in or not because we don't really know the trade-offs.

    WTD: Tell people exactly what they're getting in return for their data.

7. Best way to gain customers' trust is to be popular.

    How do you become a trusted brand? Incentives? Celebrities? Fonts? It's simpler than that (and harder): have happy customers. Some surveys show a direct correlation (download required) between trust and satisfaction.

    WTD: Do your job well, and trust will follow.

8. Marketers and consumers see the world (very) differently.

    It's natural for employees of a company (or agency) to assume their customers are like them—but that's a projection. Consumers can find personalization "creepy," while marketers assume it makes them feel "valued." Who's right?

    WTD: Don't assume anything about your customer without checking.

9. The most valuable customer-related investment is often ana-lytics.

    The Duke CMO Survey showed a spike in spending analytics on analytics. CMOs said they anticipate analytics' share of the marketing budget will grow from 6% in 2020 to 14.5% in 3 years.

WTD: Don't skimp on data, analytics, and tools.

10. Yes, AI changes everything—but not how you think.

Of course, AI will be widely applied to customer experience. But in the short term, at least, changes are likely to be incremental: learning prompt engineering, creating copy for robots to read (i.e., SEO), and high-quantity (not quality) text generation.

WTD: Start with experiments, with a human in the loop.

11. Large language models still need refinement.

If something is available to your competitors, it's not a source of advantage. The only way to make large language models sing is to tune them on your first-party data, but this requires experts (see trend No. 8) using something like a trust framework.

WTD: Focus your GenAI team on what's unique.

12. If you don't have first-party data, there are now more ways to get it.

CX professionals are revving up their first-party collection engines, but what if you don't have a lot of it? Retailers like Walmart and Kroger are more than willing to lend you theirs. So-called retail media networks (RMNs) aren't just for retail anymore: Uber, Marriott, and your favorite airline agree.

WTD: Become an expert in the RMN space, if you need it.

13. Personalization is extending into brands.

We call this the Taylor Swift Effect, based on research we've done. Why is Swift the most valuable brand on the planet? In part because she's all things to all people: a cat lover to cat lovers, a dog lover to dog lovers, a football fan to—well, bad example. But you get the idea.

WTD: Make your brand flexible enough to adapt to all the "tribes" out there.

14. Every business is now in show business.

Toys are in the movie business; energy drinks are sports promoters; even our employer, a B2B software company,

(continued)

(continued)

launched its own streaming channel. Candy bars have "Limited Editions" and spin-offs and Christmas specials. To keep customers' fragmented attention, we can all learn from the dream factory.

WTD: The first master marketer was P. T. Barnum. Enough said.

Most of these themes point to a similar response: winning customer experience needs more first-party data gathered with consent.

Old labels ("OK boomer") and methods (surveys) don't work as well, so smart companies will rely more on behavioral and real-time data and advanced analytics. AI has unlimited potential but requires guardrails to make it useful. And the importance of unstructured data like text and video is going to grow, requiring new databases and models.

For savvy companies with their eyes wide open to changes in consumer behavior and technology, there's never been a better time to jump the trends.

***

CHAPTER 6

What Do Companies Need Right Now?

Now we'll turn our attention to the other side of the register and focus on *companies*—their challenges, hopes, priorities, resources, and constraints. Most of them are aware of the listed consumer forces and are trying to adapt, but they face significant internal and external strictures on their Customer 360.

The most common Customer 360–limiting factors cited by companies include the following:

- Suboptimal technology and tools
- Technical debt and prior decisions
- Complex data types and sources
- Teams that are underprepared or under-resourced
- Corporate structures that are not aligned
- Lack of training and knowledge

Meanwhile, the so-called Vs of big data continue apace, as the Volume, Velocity, Variety of data continue to ramp. One alarming study estimated that the number of data interactions per connected person per day is growing even faster than we think. (See Figure 6.1.)

Internally, data sources expanded to store and process all this information. According to research from Salesforce, the average number of *significant* sources of customer data used by the typical enterprise doubled from under 10 in 2021 to more than 20 in 2024, with no end in sight.

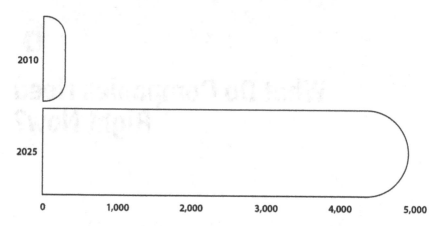

FIGURE 6.1 Data Interactions per Person per Day (#)

Most companies' ultimate goal is to provide a customer experience that is better than competitors and not only meets but delights customers' rising expectations. Fully 82% of higher-performing organizations agree that CX is a key source of competitive differentiation.

THE PERCEPTION-REALITY CHASM

A few years ago, the technology consulting firm Capgemini released a compelling study quantifying the relationship between customer experience and net promoter score.[1] (Net promoter score, or NPS, is a commonly used benchmark of self-reported customer satisfaction.) Not surprisingly, the researchers found a clear correlation between better perceived experiences and NPS and proved an economic benefit.

Consumers showed significantly higher "willingness to spend" driven by a better experience. Specifically, the Capgemini data showed a six point increase in customer experience (i.e., a 60% higher relative score) led to a 6x or 600% increase in willingness to spend. There's a real payoff to improving your customers' lives.

Unfortunately, a big gap still exists between companies' perceptions of their own abilities here and the reality on the ground. A different study found that while an impressive 75% of organizations believed they were "customer-centric," only 30% of consumers agreed. The size of this perception-reality gap differs by industry and region. Utilities had the biggest rift, while digital-native brands such as newer e-commerce players enjoyed the smallest perception gap. As usual, consumers in Europe were the least impressed, while those in Asia-Pacific were happiest.

DATA VARIETY AND MANAGEMENT

Not long ago, at the height of the vogue for data lakes, the industry analyst firm Gartner started to warn clients of the dangers of "dark data." Dark data are objects that exist (somewhere) in the labyrinth of corporate data stores with no real reason to be and no reliable means of access. Gartner was warning against the dangers of data over-collection without forethought.

Yet over-collection is not the only danger. One recent survey of enterprise data professionals indicated that about 56% of relevant customer data isn't captured at all, even as 43% of the data *that is captured* is not used. So there are two sides to the data dynamic: an undoubted tendency to over-capture and store unnecessary information (i.e., data that's never used for analytics or operations) and also a tendency not to collect important information from customers that *could* be used.

As we saw in our 14 megatrends in the previous chapter, video is an increasingly critical customer channel. Yet it points to a problem: unstructured data, which can make up the majority of an enterprises' store, are often not available for use. Call center transcripts; pre-produced, live-streamed, interactive and user-generated video, text, and images; PDF documents and internal meeting transcripts; customer survey feedback and chatbot dialogues; commissioned research transcripts—much of this unstructured data are not yet part of the customer data analysts' arsenal.

More than 90% of companies report increasing their use of video in recent years, and the penetration of livestream video production jumped from 73% to almost 90%. Meanwhile, the use of influencer marketing (which generates its own unstructured data) rose from 66% to 73%.

Economic factors impact an organizations' ability to support the proliferation of data types and sources. Each year, Duke's Fuqua School of Business releases a comprehensive benchmark survey of chief marketing officers, in collaboration with the American Marketing Association and Deloitte. A survey released in 2023 showed that CMO's, at least, were tempering spending due to economic concerns.[2]

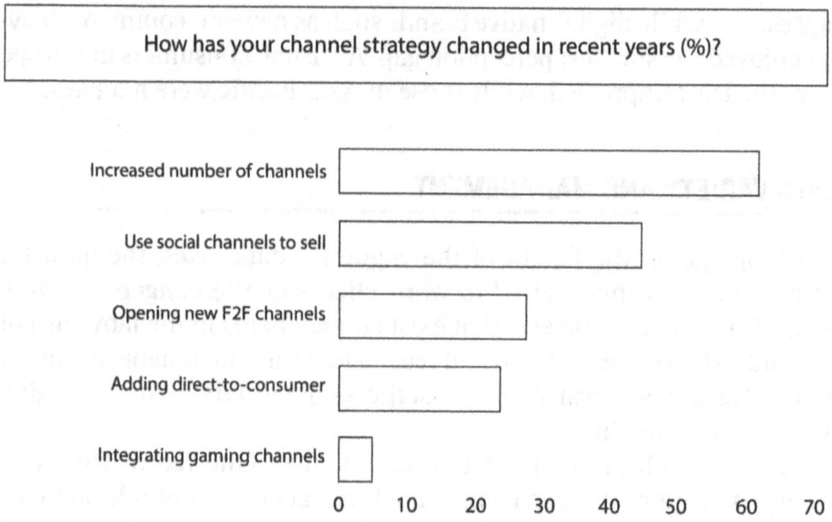

How has your channel strategy changed in recent years (%)?

FIGURE 6.2   Change in Channel Strategy (%)

In fact, the Duke survey showed that the combination of pandemic-related retooling and economic risks continued to affect both tactics and strategy. In addition to encouraging efficiency, these forces were moving many respondents to *increase* spending in direct-to-consumer and one-to-one channels. (See Figure 6.2.)

THE CUSTOMER EXPERIENCE TECH STACK

We'll have much more to say on the tech stack and its role in the Customer 360 in Chapter 9. For now, let's touch on a few salient points from our market survey. We can sum it up like this: companies of all sizes face a bewildering array of applications and data sources, and they (understandably) fear that they are not rising to the challenge.

Estimates vary, but a reasonable 2024 estimate from Zylo showed the following:[3]

- SMBs with 500 or fewer employees: 162 applications (average)
- Mid-market companies with 501–2,500 employees: 245 applications
- Larger companies: 900+ applications (MuleSoft estimate)

That's a lot of applications, many of which contain trapped customer data: information about the same customer that isn't easily accessible and hasn't been unified with other data about that same customer into a workable profile.

Not surprisingly, almost two-thirds of companies report that they rely at least partly on manual data integration when trying to manage all these applications across channels. And one-third admitted their data management teams spent at least 25% of their time—one full week every month—simply wrangling data (collecting, cleansing). That's time spent doing data plumbing rather than analysis and action.

PRIORITIES AND INVESTMENTS

Setting priorities is a precursor to investment decisions, and priorities are informed both by an awareness of existing challenges and the strategic assessment of opportunities and ways to grow. That's why we so often see in survey data that challenges and priorities are highly correlated. And right at the top of the stack in both realms are technology, tools, and analytics.

In one global survey, customer experience managers are asked each year to rank their top current challenges—the things that keep them up at night—and their top priorities for the coming year. It's an interesting snapshot of the Customer 360 professional's psyche.

Top Challenges

1. Ineffective use of tools and technologies
2. Measuring ROI and attribution
3. Balancing personalization with customer comfort levels (i.e., the "creepy factor")
4. Building and retaining trust with customers
5. Resistance to new strategies and tactics (i.e., team pushback)

Top Priorities

1. Improving the use of tools and technologies
2. Experimenting with new strategies and tactics
3. Modernizing tools and technologies
4. Building and retaining trust with customers
5. Improving collaboration across teams

A clear theme emerging from this and other reports is that *tools and technologies* are seen as both an enabler and a source of stress, something that has potential to make life better (because it does) but also requires significant investments in resources, talent, and time. Meanwhile, our CX professionals have to keep the business running. Nobody said Customer 360 was easy.

A broader survey of technology professionals revealed a similar, more pointed short list of top challenges: that they "can't keep pace" with customers' expectations (57%) and with the evolving tech landscape; that they won't be able to integrate new technologies with existing systems; a plethora of disparate platforms; and, finally, a poor user experience with their tools (user interface (UI)/user experience (UX)).

Those companies investing in new CX technologies are generally happy. One survey showed that 60% of companies investing in digital customer engagement technologies had already improved their ability to meet changing customer needs, and 90% said such engagement increased revenue (up from 70% 2 years ago). Not surprisingly, companies said they planned to double their investment in real-time personalization technologies in the next 2–3 years.

One consultancy, in collaboration with the Interactive Advertising Bureau (IAB), released an updated State of Data report in 2024.[4] In addition to showing more than $12 billion in spending by companies on different types of data (demographic, transactional, behavioral, location-based), the report showed that companies were also increasing spend on two forms of data processing:

- Data management: $5.5 billion
- Analytics: $2.4 billion

Overall spending on data management and processing is growing at a faster rate than analytics (15% growth rate for the former, compared to about 3%). This is no surprise given the complexity spurt just outlined.

But even these impressive numbers dissolve in the rearview mirror as we race toward the AI software boom. Spending on AI software is projected to be around $300 billion by 2027, growing 20% to 30% yearly.

FIRST-PARTY DATA AND PRIVACY

As we've seen, virtually all consumers claim they want "more control" over their personal data, with a priority on control over their identity data (e.g., personally identifiable information [PII] like phone numbers, emails, addresses, etc.). So it makes sense that a large majority of companies (89%) say they already or imminently plan to implement strategies for first- and zero-party data privacy.

Efforts continue across industries and markets to collect more customer data and to better manage new and existing data. Over the past 18 months, 57% of companies report having increased their use of first-party and contextual data. And more than one in three report making a significant effort to centralize customer data.

Yet challenges with first-party data abound. Companies may want more—so they can deliver a better experience, among other uses—but consumers have a perfect right to say no, expect guardrails and options, and to change their minds. There's also the fact that customer data is not something many enterprises have mastered yet.

In descending order, the most often-cited challenges with first-party data were the following:

- Ensuring privacy and security
- Consumer resistance to providing it
- Lack of internal technical skills
- Lack of relevant technologies and tools
- Poor data quality

"Privacy is a fundamental human right."
—Tim Cook, CEO, Apple

***

In this section, we introduced the concept of Customer 360 and outlined its key pillars of Data + AI + Trust. We presented a fast-moving case study in Formula 1 and suggested the various ways it's possible to gain value from improving customer experience. We then introduced the Five Forces of Customer Experience, our CX-driven homage to Michael Porter.

LET'S REVISIT THESE FORCES FOR A MOMENT

As you can see, the previous two chapters—where we talked about the current state of customers, and the challenges and priorities of companies—were addressing the x-axis: (Customer) Expectations lead

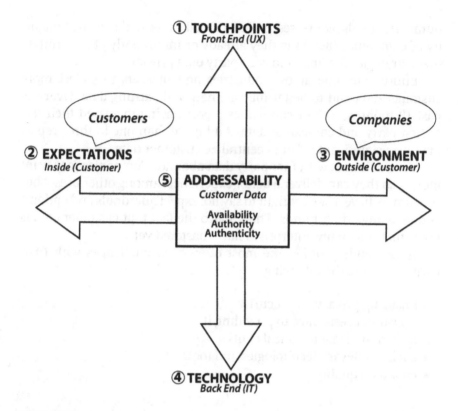

FIGURE 6.3   The Five Forces of Customer 360

to (Company) Environment. Of course, we can only make a start here but hope we have provided some inspiration.

But what about the *y*-axis— the one dealing with technology and data? Well, that's what the rest of this book is about. In the following section, we'll talk directly about the customer experience tech stack, how it's evolved and where it's going. We'll address how the customer data platform has evolved to support the entire Customer 360 from end to end. And we'll cover key topics like composability, collaboration, and consent; what "real-time" really means; and (of course) analytics and AI.

Finally, in Section 3, we'll address the critical issue of the human factor—how people can be upskilled, reskilled, organized, and inspired to propel an organization into the nexus of Customer 360.

***

SECTION
Two

DATA + AI + TRUST IN ACTION

CHAPTER 7

The Evolution of Customer Data and Platforms—A Case Study

I n this chapter, we will follow the evolution of a single company as it developed its own approach to the Customer 360. Today it offers a single platform with the components needed for a successful end-to-end customer experience. This company is Salesforce.

We would never say there is only one approach to building a Customer 360. Realistically, enterprise tech stacks will always host components from dozens—often hundreds—of different vendors combined with homegrown and agency- and consultant-built tools. Experts like Scott Brinker, known as @chiefmartec, make a compelling case that dramatic vendor consolidation is neither imminent nor even necessary.

We'll focus on Salesforce because it has the advantage of global scale, cross-industry focus, market success, and a comprehensive Customer 360 offering. (Full disclosure: another advantage is that both the authors work there, so it's familiar.) But we'd like to be clear that Salesforce is not the only vendor making important contributions in this space.

THE SALESFORCE STORY

Salesforce.com was launched in 1999 at the height of the internet boom in the Valley—a time when adding a dot-com to a company's name marked it as a challenger. Two dogs and four cofounders, including Marc Benioff and Parker Harris, set to work in a one-bedroom apartment on the top of San Francisco's Telegraph Hill, spiritually supervised by posters of the Dalai Lama and Albert Einstein.

Its original idea was to deliver customer relationship management (CRM) software via a cloud subscription model later known as SaaS (software-as-a-service). Ubiquitous today, SaaS was seen at the time as risky and untried, even threatening to some IT departments that had only known on-premises products. The argument for SaaS was that—as the code was maintained on the vendor's servers and delivered over the internet—it eliminated a lot of manual installation and maintenance and delivered continual updates. It could also be "rented" by the month and easily canceled.

A tagline on its original website, designed to look like Amazon.com, read: "Exploit the Power of the Internet to Harness Your Sales Information!" It elaborated: ". . . Easily access, manage, and/or share all your organization's sales information—immediately, efficiently and reliably—right from your computer."

The company grew quickly, in part due to dramatic events. Its launch party at the Regency Hotel in San Francisco set a tone: there was a lower level labeled Hell, featuring games of whack-a-mole (the moles were other software vendors). Upstairs was Heaven, branded with a "No Software" theme ("software" meaning clunky on-premise products). By 2003, an annual event tradition called Dreamforce was launched at the Westin St. Francis Hotel in San Francisco.

Within 2 years, the company reached $20 million revenue and was at $100 million in 2004, when it went public. It was making $1 billion by 2008 and $35 billion in 2024. Obviously, SaaS wasn't the only reason for the company's rising fortunes. Other early technical decisions were critical.

One design choice was particularly decisive, in retrospect. CRM began with sales force automation, providing tools for business-to-business (B2B) sales people to keep track of leads, contacts, accounts, and opportunities. Parker Harris and his technical team decided to use a metadata model to ensure consistency. In simple terms, standard data objects were created—commonly used entities such as Contact (a person with a role related to an Account), or Opportunity (a particular sales process related to a Product and an Account). These objects were structured using *metadata* that ensured each individual piece of data had a label.

For example, "FirstName" might be the metadata that labeled a data field containing a first name. Keeping these labels consistent across all the data that flowed through the system made it flexible. New features and applications could be built and would work with what came before. Salesforce launched Service Cloud in 2009 and quickly became a leading call-center software player in large part because Service Cloud used the same metadata model as Sales Cloud, the original Salesforce automation application.

We've said that a Customer 360 approach requires a platform. What's a platform? It's a consistent set of technical services that allow other services to operate and interoperate. ("Service" here just means a computer program that performs a useful function.) As early as 2003, Salesforce launched Sforce2.0, described as the "industry's first on-demand application service." Two years later, it launched the AppExchange, which was a marketplace of approved applications that could plug into and enhance the users' CRM; *Forbes* called it the "iTunes of business software." (See Figure 7.1.)

FIGURE 7.1   Early Salesforce.com Homepage

Harris wanted to make it easier for external applications, including highly customized homegrown code, to work with the platform. AppExchange was one step, providing a way for vendors and even customers to build and offer their apps in an open marketplace. Another step was the Apex programming language, announced in 2006, which effectively allowed third-parties (customers, partners, developers) to run their own code inside Salesforce. The introduction of VisualForce (user interface [UI] elements) and Force.com a few years later meant that these third parties could basically build their own apps directly on Salesforce, access objects and metadata, and design their own UIs.

Subsequent years expanded the platform into channels like mobile (Salesforce1); added capabilities like machine learning and AI (Einstein); and unified the look and feel around plug-and-play design elements (Lightning). Major acquisitions added platform capabilities such as large-scale data integration (MuleSoft), data analysis and visualization (Tableau), and collaboration (Slack).

THE EMERGENCE OF DATA CLOUD

The foundation of any Customer 360 is data. Common objects and metadata provide a way to structure data within a platform. Identifiers like ContactID are needed to link different data points to a single Contact (or person). But what about all those other customer-related applications and IDs that are sitting in the enterprise's many applications that *are not* on the particular vendors (e.g., Salesforce's) platform? How can anyone hope to assemble all of these into a coherent Customer 360 that treats the entire customer experience from end to end?

Starting around 2008, once Salesforce's platform-as-a-service (PaaS) was established, the company began to think about how to improve its users' access to customer data sitting outside its own platform. Service Cloud was launched with externally managed unique IDs that could link data across applications. But its customers' data architectures were getting more and more complex all the time.

The reality on the ground was that many companies had invested millions in master data management, ETL (extract-transform-load) and enterprise data warehouses, and data marts; and they often had discrete systems for data resolution, linking and management functions such as profiling, cleansing, enrichment, integration, and reporting. All these different systems typically needed manual, homegrown, point-to-point integrations that were often brittle and slow. Adding the Salesforce platform to this mix did not magically unleash all the customer data. (See Figure 7.2.)

An interim solution was Data.com (originally Jigsaw), a source of structured data about accounts and leads that could be updated by a user community. (Data.com was phased out in 2020.) Salesforce also came up with a common data architecture for customers. The CRM platform would house separate self-service "views" of Accounts and Products, as well as a Sales and Service view in the applications. Back-office data such as sales and shipments could be integrated manually. But once Salesforce got into the business-to-consumer (B2C) world with its launch of Marketing Cloud, it became clear that a more automated solution was needed to handle the ever-growing data volume.

Typically, coordinating customer data across systems in the enterprise was the domain of master data management (MDM). In addition to head-spinning complexity, MDM could take years to implement. Salesforce's customer research revealed that what business users wanted was not really a new "golden record"—something that was a 100% reliable reference for every piece of customer data—but rather a customer profile that was up-to-date, flexible, and had the data needed for the job, whether that was customer service, offer generation, website personalization, etc.

So it developed something called Customer 360 Data Manager. Customer 360 Data Manager was a framework that allowed data about the same customer or account, sitting in different data stores, to be linked to a common ID. This was not an easily accessible real-time profile of all the data available about that customer or account; it was just an ID linkage. But it was the critical first step.

At this time—as described in more detail in our book *Customer Data Platforms*—the customer data platform (CDP) market was growing quickly, essentially to solve the same scattered-ID and disparate-data problem. However, first-generation CDPs were generally limited to marketing use cases, marketing users, and common marketing data sources. They did not even try to solve the end-to-end Customer 360 problem yet.

Salesforce's first step into the CDP space was Customer 360 Audiences, released in 2019. It sat alongside and relied on Customer 360 Data Manager. Where the latter was an ID manager and system of reference for the customer profile, Customer 360 Audiences was designed to be a source of truth, primarily for marketing data. Built on a hyperscale Data Lake that could handle millions of customer profiles (that is, B2C scale), it included tools to ingest data from outside

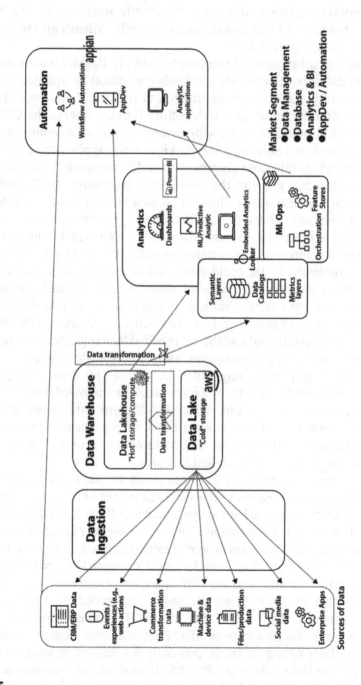

FIGURE 7.2 Example Enterprise Customer Data Stack

sources, do segmentation and analytics, and activate audiences to outside systems like email and advertising.

Customer 360 Audiences was later renamed Salesforce Customer Data Platform (to avoid category confusion). By 2023, it was officially moved out from under the Marketing Cloud umbrella and was renamed Salesforce Data Cloud. So it remains today. It is the fastest growing organic product in Salesforce history and probably the fastest growing software product ever to reach $200 million and then $300 million (and beyond) in run rate revenue.

Essentially, Data Cloud releases customer and account data that are trapped in different applications and databases in the organization. It does this by providing all of the services that an enterprise CDP provides, with an important distinction: it is explicitly designed for the entire Customer 360, from advertising and marketing through customer service, in-store clienteling, loyalty, e-commerce, sales, business intelligence, and more.

DATA CLOUD ARCHITECTURE

As you would expect, under the hood Data Cloud uses the Salesforce platform metadata, packaging, extensibility, user experience (Lightning), and the AppExchange. What it added was the ability to handle true B2C big data scale and computation requirements, which meant building a secure Data Lake on top of public cloud infrastructure providers such as Amazon Web Services.

Data Cloud has three layers: (1) a data plane, which is the storage layer; (2) a compute plane, where data are processed and transformed; and (3) a stream processing and query plane, which is where streaming (real-time) data flows and queries are directed. The storage layer contains metadata and the data itself. The compute processes include data processing (Spark, Iceberg, etc.), transformations (mapping data to data models, for harmonization), and other services such as identity resolution and segmentation.

Like all such systems, Data Cloud functions at a number of different speeds. It uses a Lakehouse architecture for storage, which maintains objects at various levels of refinement. These range from raw data, which are retained, to transformed and mapped data ready for use. It also has the facility to ingest streaming data (e.g., APIs through

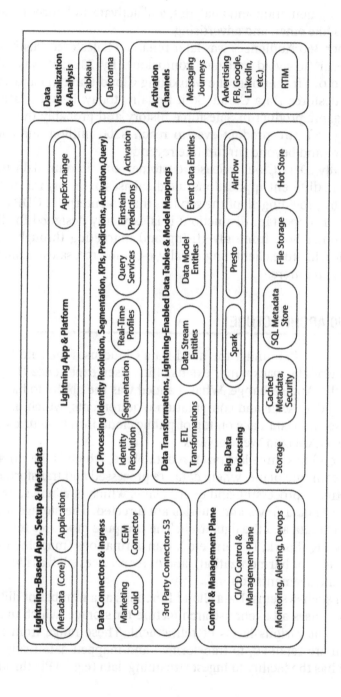

FIGURE 7.3 Data Cloud High-level Architecture

58

Kafka), which can trigger downstream actions, often based on changes in data—for example, if a person shifts loyalty status, or opens a case. (We'll talk more about real-time data in Chapter 11.)

Data Cloud is the data element of Customer 360, and it is embedded within a larger structure called the Einstein 1 Platform, which includes the other elements of AI + Trust. Recall that Salesforce's applications (Sales Cloud, Service Cloud, etc.) use the same metadata framework. Therefore Data Cloud functions as a unified profile of customer and account data, including data from these applications, as well as data from external vendors, databases, and other sources.

Salesforce started an AI research team in 2014, launched its Einstein ML/AI-supporting portfolio 2 years later, and created an Office of Ethical & Humane use in 2018. With the advent of more powerful GenAI and open-source models in 2022, Salesforce began building out its Einstein Trust Layer. The purpose of this layer is to give users of its platform access to external models such as OpenAI and Google's Gemini—but with enterprise-ready features to ensure a useful output.

These features include toxicity and bias detection, the masking of personal data, enhanced security, and the ability to ground or retrain models based on first-party data. So Salesforce's open platform—at the level of data, storage, and UI—is also open at the level of AI model building.

KEY ELEMENTS OF A CUSTOMER 360 PLATFORM

Salesforce developed a customer experience platform over the past 2 decades by focusing on a handful of design principles. Some were there from the start, and others were introduced over time. Whether they use Salesforce or not, any enterprise can learn from the company's approach to building a platform that's well positioned to support the entire Customer 360.

These principles are the following:

1. *Cloud hyperscalers:* Salesforce started in the cloud before AWS and Google Cloud Services, when private clouds were standard. With the introduction of Hyperforce (Salesforce on public cloud) and Data Cloud, it's moved onto the public cloud hyperscalers for scale and efficiency.

2. *Metadata:* To be interoperable, systems must use data that are somehow coded. Salesforce adopted metadata and the Cloud Information Model (CIM), a standard set of reference objects. These are also polymorphic, meaning they can be adapted to different industries.

3. *Unified UI:* Often downplayed, the UI that the user logs into each day is its portal to the tools themselves. Starting with Visualforce and then Lightning, Salesforce developed a configurable, customizable, drag-and-drop UI that's consistent.

4. *Processing speed:* Most data processes were scheduled, batch jobs until fairly recently. Now streaming data is critical to a superior customer experience; customers *expect* at least some profile data to be updated in real time. For example, if they're asking a chatbot (or agent) questions about an item on the website, it would be nice if the call-center rep knew what they're looking at. Salesforce introduced Data Graphs and other capabilities to enhance its real-time support.

5. *Trust:* Scale and security were always important. Improvements in the power of third-party AI means that many customers want to use them to enhance their customer experience. However, they can't be used in a corporate setting without strict guardrails and features like data grounding. The latter is a way of customizing large public models on first-party data to make them more useful in specific contexts, like service and marketing.

6. *Einstein:* ML and AI are not features but capabilities, and enterprises need a range of options from prebuilt plug-ins to AI-driven copilots to data science support. Salesforce added pipelines to data science tools like Amazon Sagemaker and Google Vertex to Data Cloud.

We acknowledge that Salesforce is not the only road to the rainbow, but it provides a good example of a company that's building a platform capable of supporting the breadth and depth of the Customer 360. Built on pillars of flexibility, interoperability, configurability and scale, Salesforce shows us some of the prerequisites for success.

No single vendor could ever make up the entirety of an enterprise's tech stack—nor is such a monolith a good idea. How does a Customer 360 platform fit within the modern enterprise, given all its legacy and custom solutions, operational complexity, and strategic firestorms? After touching on the key issue of data types and formats, we'll move onto the all-important question of how various technologies fit together to support the customer experience.

***

CHAPTER 8

Data Types and Sources

Let's get back into the heart of our Five Forces of Customer Experience and focus further on data before exploring the *y*-axis in more detail. In this chapter, we will examine types and sources of data that are critical to target and leverage in order to enrich your Customer 360 activations. Of the subforces of data mentioned in Chapter 4—availability, authority and authenticity—the focus here is on the types of *available* data that are worth untrapping while addressing *authority* and *authenticity* (and AI) a bit too.

EVOLUTION OF DATA TYPES

The growth and evolution of data have fundamentally transformed how we handle and utilize them. The global volume of data is projected to reach 175 zetabytes by 2025.[1] (For context, one zetabyte is equal to 10^{21} bytes or a trillion gigabytes)

Traditional data types such as integers, floats, strings, arrays, and Boolean expressions formed the foundation for data representation in programs and databases. These highly organized data are considered "structured" data. Data from places such as social media, videos, and websites are considered "unstructured data."

The mix of structured and unstructured data is referred to as "semi-structured" data. Semi-structured data could include an image that is tagged with some label information. An email, for example, is considered semi-structured because the date and time of an email are structured data, while the email contents are unstructured. The fastest category of data growth is semi-structured due to the practice of meta tagging across documents, videos, and images to create classifications.

Raw data in context and its relation to other data are what create insights, so putting these various data together is a complex but important puzzle to solve. Roughly 80% of the data organizations create or collect is unstructured or semi-structured.[2] The challenge many companies face is categorizing these fragments of data using metadata to make the data more usable. Let's dive into the definitions of each and why this is so critical in today's market context.

	Structured	Unstructured
What is it?	Data that are highly organized, factual, and fit neatly in a database such as text, numeric, or alphanumeric	Data don't have predefined structures and come in a variety of formats such as video, audio, images, text messages, HTML, PDFs, and email content
Analysis	Quantitative	Qualitative
Storage	Requires less storage	Requires more storage due to being stored as an object in raw, large file formats
Storage format	Data warehouses and relational databases	Applications, NoSQL databases, data lakes and nonrelational databases
Data access	Accessible via spreadsheets, SQL; easy to retrieve and analyze	Advanced tools to access and analyze such as natural processing language and ML

Extracting and labeling data for use are critical challenges to fuel engagement with customers. The rush to collect these insights for use has been exacerbated by the advent of GenAI. Companies want to have reliable data on which to train their models. (We talk more about AI in Chapter 12.) The rapid proliferation of complex and diverse data has led to the need for handling, storing, and processing data to become more efficient. The ability to put these structured, unstructured, and semi-structured data pieces together into a clearer picture of your target audiences is a key competitive advantage.

DATA STORAGE

Companies traditionally stored data in relational databases, which are ideal for handling structured data with defined rows and columns and useful when the volume of data is manageable. A data warehouse is a specialized type of database designed for processing structured data for analytical processing and reporting. However, as data volume grew, and semi-structured data became more prevalent, traditional relational databases couldn't handle the growing complexity. Furthermore, the abundance of unstructured data in the form of documents, recordings, social media content, or videos presented even more data from disparate places.

Data lakes emerged to better handle the vast amount of semi-structured and structured data. Also, they provide the scalability, flexibility, and the ability to ingest, process, and store data. The data lake house combines the analytics flexibility of a data warehouse with the advanced analytics of data lakes and ability to handle the range of data types. Data lakes are still a common area of investment for IT buyers today. (See Figure 8.1.)

Today an emerging market for data storage and management is referred to as data fabric. Data fabric is a data management approach that provides a consistent, unified architecture to access structured and unstructured data regardless of where they are stored. The core concept is providing central access to data for a business through services and technologies that enable data-driven decisions via self-service. Fabric also helps with other data management requirements, such as data integration, cataloging, orchestration, data lineage, data governance, and access. A good example would be the ability to have

	Data Warehouse Early 1990's	Data Lake Early 2010's	Data Lakehouse Early 2020's	Data Fabric Early 2020's
Usage	• Descriptive • Reports and dashboards	• Predictive • Reports, analytics, machine learning	• Predictive and generative • Real-time analytics	• Prescriptive • Harmonized view across your data ecosystem using existing tools together
Primary audiences	• Business intelligence, data analysts	• Business intelligence, data analysts • Data scientists • Machine learning	• Business intelligence, advanced data analysts • Data scientists • Machine learning	• Everyone including line of business leaders
Scope	• Centralized data storage and management • Standardized data format – structured data	• Centralized data storage and management • Multiple data formats – structured, semi-structured, and unstructured	• Centralized data storage • Supports structured, semi-structured, and unstructured data – image, audio, video	• Distributed storage • Multiple data formats – structured and unstructured including data at rest and in-flight • Automation for data mgmt and preparation
Implications	• Ideal for historical analysis • Data volume constraints • Time consuming to extract, transform, load (ETL) to import data	• Scalability • Getting insights out of this data is huge effort • Lack of support for concurrent transactions • Lack of data governance	• Scalability • Ability to accelerate data processing • Improved performance • Simplified Integrations • Robust governance	• Adaptive analytics, real-time business operations • Analytics in the flow of work • Shift focus from hindsight to foresight / predictive / anticipatory / proactive

FIGURE 8.1 The Evolution of Data Management

a harmonized view of your data across your operational apps without impacting daily operations. This also provides an easy way to prepare and package data for AI.

Instead of "boiling the ocean" and solving for trapped data in aggregate, we suggest companies determine what data they should prioritize to get the most important pieces of the puzzle together first. Curating the right data is key to generating the fact-base that will prioritize how you invest your money to maximize operational efficiency and grow your business.

Roughly speaking, customer data comes in four types.

TYPICAL CUSTOMER DATA TYPES

1. Demographic data: Foundational customer background data such as age, gender, education, address, telephone number, etc. This provides baseline insights about customers, allowing companies to personalize and segment relevant interactions and experiences.
2. Transactional data: Records of customers' transactions, including purchase orders, payments, returns, or preorders. These data are key for understanding customer's buying patterns, interests, or even return patterns. They help businesses to understand whether these customers are bargain shoppers, loyalists, impulsive buyers, or social shoppers. Also, these data are key to identifying how your products are working, how effective your pricing strategy is, and what categories are resonating.
3. Behavioral data: Website visits, clicks, social media visits, email open rates, purchase patterns, service, and product usage. Analyzing behavioral in real time or near real time provides businesses with the insights into customer preferences to make critical customer engagement experiences in the moment. These data provide the intelligence that fosters brand loyalty and customer retention.
4. Firmographic data: Company name, address, industry, headquarters, number of employees, or financial metrics. This information is specific to a company and is used in account-based marketing (ABM) for B2B experiences.

Consumer expectations and business needs have evolved around the growing importance of real-time insights and responses.

This necessitated the adoption of real-time data streaming and event-driven architectures. These technologies enable immediate responses to events, real-time monitoring, and the detection of patterns, anomalies, and insights from streaming data sources. Organizations using real-time data capabilities gain a competitive edge by making data-driven decisions in the moment, enhancing consumer experiences, and optimizing operations.

For example, if you are a retailer, you can imagine a consumer on your mobile app browsing certain products online that use a barcode for a promotion in your store. Based on this consumer's past behavior and purchasing patterns, she is most likely a college student and is likely returning for the school year. You also bring in data from a real-time weather feed. A marketer may use these data to create an effective campaign that offers a timely, relevant promotional offer for a back-to-school sale on shorts and sandals.

Customers benefit from coordinated interactions with brands when their data are centralized for use across the Customer 360. Customers on service calls with problems can have faster, more responsive experiences if their commerce history and reaction to past marketing campaigns are used to provide the right proactive service experience in the moment. Perhaps a customer that was about to churn will be recovered and converted into a loyal customer.

Eventually it may not matter whether the front door to this experience was marketing, service, or commerce as they are all centered on the same goal: a customer benefitting from a coordinated, personalized, and positive experience with your business. In the previous shorts and sandals example, does it matter if it was marketing or commerce for the win? In the service call, saving a customer from attriting saves on the marketing spend needed for a new customer acquisition.

THE DATA PARTY

Data sources are also defined by how the data were collected and whether the information was shared willingly with the recipient company or not. (While there are differences in taxonomy, we'll stick to zero- through third-party data here.) Zero-party data are the most straightforward because people have voluntarily shared the information with a business. They have "opted-into" and usually received

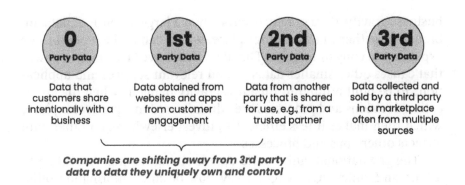

0 Party Data	1st Party Data	2nd Party Data	3rd Party Data
Data that customers share intentionally with a business	Data obtained from websites and apps from customer engagement	Data from another party that is shared for use, e.g., from a trusted partner	Data collected and sold by a third party in a marketplace often from multiple sources

Companies are shifting away from 3rd party data to data they uniquely own and control

FIGURE 8.2 Data Types by Source

some benefit in return. When customers complete a post-sale survey product review, they may receive a promotion or incentive. They may expect the company to also act on the positive or negative feedback provided. (See Figure 8.2.)

First-party data provide behavioral signals, such as product interests, purchasing history, and download data. Businesses often "own" and have a right to leverage their zero- and first-party data for personalizing engagements. As demands for consumer privacy and regulations increase, businesses are learning to rely less on nonconsented third-party data. In subsequent chapters we discuss third-party cookie deprecation and the likely rise of second-party data through new data sharing and collaboration technologies.

DATA AND BUSINESS GRAVITY

Bringing your critical customer data together to empower your business is key whether you are using a CDP or a more general-purpose, enterprise-wide holistic data technology such as a data warehouse, data lake, or a data fabric as the foundation. But once that data are combined, how do you ensure the information is actionable? Are marketers and customer service reps logging into their data lake to get a campaign sent to a segmented audience? Which of these disparate data systems are relevant and the highest priority?

Two forces are at play that have shaped the management of data for use in the Customer 360 over the past year: data gravity and business gravity. Data gravity occurs when a large amount of data are brought together in a particular place, which can make it onerous or expensive to copy or migrate. That data then have an attractive power that causes other smaller datasets and relevant services and applications to be built around it. Business gravity happens when the application decisions and processes are administered in a particular place, which then makes it less efficient to invest elsewhere, and therefore attracts other apps and processes.

The gravitational pull around data is strengthening. According to a Morgan Stanley 4Q23 CIO Survey, 40% of chief information officers anticipate consolidating database and data storage vendors within 3 years.[3] Within 12 months, 45% plan to use either a third-party cloud data warehouse or a native public cloud such as Amazon Redshift or Google BigQuery. In practice, this means that some line of business buyers choosing the apps they want to use for marketing or commerce will need to fit in or connect into the company's overarching data strategy. Reducing silos is step one, so the next step is to figure out the apps and tactics for marketers and commerce executives to unlock that data for use.

While warehouses and data lakes offer data gravity, customer-facing applications are uniquely positioned to support business gravity and the line of business owners responsible for the end-user experience. Business gravity centers around having the needed UI and the business control panel to orchestrate, act, and analyze results. This interface is critical whether it is a human activating experiences manually or a human at the helm overseeing AI to get the job done.

The source data can be brought into your company's data warehouse, data lake, or CDP via various methods, which include streaming real-time data, batch ingestion, and bidirectional federated query. Some of the common sources of data leading to actionable customer profile intelligence include the following:

- Marketing automation applications
- Service CRM
- Sales CRM
- Commerce applications
- Loyalty management applications
- Retail point-of-sale (POS)
- Order management

- Data management platform (DMP)
- Social advertising platforms
- Web content management systems (CMS)
- Enterprise resource planning (ERP)
- Internet of things (IoT)

The Salesforce Research & Insights team introduced us to their hypothesis around a third force that sits between data and business gravity—knowledge gravity. In this middle ground, technologies exist to manage intelligence infrastructure such as business logic and metadata, modeling and model operations, and monitoring and analytics.

Today, CDPs that have a data lake house structure like Salesforce Data Cloud fit this definition because of their ability to federate data bidirectionally (without duplicating data) from existing data infrastructure investments or any of the data sources listed earlier via native connectors or application programming interfaces (APIs). (We will talk about data federation, sharing, and collaboration in Chapter 14.). AI and ML operations hubs could ultimately reside in any one of these three locations, a combination of two, or all. (See Figure 8.3.)

Applying this heuristic, it is easy to see that a CDP built on the architecture of a lake house with multiple data sources and destinations is not fully realized as a marketing-only tool. The CDP category itself is clearly durable: invented in 2013, it still applies to a highly heterogeneous group of vendors.

In the future, it's possible that vendors whose products are still only offering marketing activations could be renamed "marketing

FIGURE 8.3 Three Types of Enterprise Gravity

data platforms." In any case, CDPs that have a data lake or lake house foundation and strong connectivity to data, as well as a range of business UI destinations, are ideally suited to support knowledge gravity. In this context, a Customer 360 intelligence-to-action capability would deliver better total cost of ownership than a marketing data platform.

EXAMPLES OF UNTRAPPED DATA IN ACTION

In our equation of Data + AI + Trust, Data is the foundation. And we've made the case here that Data is only really useful when freed from its original application-specific context and combined into unified customer profiles. In this way, trapped data are "freed" to support the three forces of gravity. These data can take many forms across industries, three of which are featured next.

Electronic vehicle manufacturer: For example, a car manufacturer may want to study key product features that customers are (and aren't) using in their electric cars to (1) send personalized messaging to drivers related to their vehicle or (2) prioritize future areas of innovation. In this instance, the car's telemetry data combined with audience demographics and driving patterns could provide insights that would be missed if the various data sources remained trapped.

Today, it's an advantage to think of ways to engage customers beyond the traditional lens of marketers. Every service experience can also be a marketing and loyalty opportunity. Every commerce purchase experience should be a great service experience. Purchasing information can be used to tailor relevant marketing communications, and so on.

Financial services company: Banco Inter is Brazil's first 100% digital bank, a pioneer in the country's financial landscape. Inter offers free checking, personal, corporate, and microenterprise accounts; loans and credit cards; and investment and insurance services.

In 3 years of high growth, Inter's customer data started to spread across six different sources and 103 streams. Each customer might own multiple products, leading to duplicate records and irrelevant messages. Inter needed to connect with customers on a more personal level by uniting marketing campaign data, sales transactional data, and web and mobile behavioral data in a single view. As a pioneer in digital banking, Inter also wanted to lead the way in AI while managing risk and data privacy.

Inter implemented a CDP to unify key data sources, which enabled it to create more complete customer profiles that were segmented into audiences. With this unified view of customers, Inter was able to improve the efficacy of marketing communications while also eliminating an average of 1.5 hours of meetings per person per day. Inter also uses a business intelligence tool to instantly analyze customer profiles and their preferences to generate an engagement score for each customer. By making each experience more personal, Inter increased conversion rates 35 times and overall return on investment 20 times.

Inter is also using GenAI built on a collaboration platform to make teams more productive using InterGPT. Now, more than 1,000 Inter developers write and review product code in any development language. Also, making AI accessible to users in the flow of work enables product recommendations and next-best-action results. Service employees can use the app to answer customer questions and translate responses an average of 30 minutes faster per month.

Storage and information management services company: Iron Mountain is an American enterprise information management services company supporting more than 96% of Fortune 1000 companies. Iron Mountain's records management, information destruction, and data backup and recovery services are supplied to more than 240,000 customers in 60+ countries throughout the globe.

Before, Iron Mountain's service agents had to switch between multiple apps and databases to gather enough context for each customer's order or inquiry. The order process was manual, and information was located in different places, forcing agents to swivel between different systems. Agents also had to search the knowledge base manually, resulting in long lead times and a growing backlog of inquiries. Despite massive amounts of customer data, agents couldn't easily access it and use it meaningfully.

Now, with MuleSoft integrating various pieces of the puzzle, Salesforce provides a single service platform to help agents create a connected experience across email, chat, and voice. When customers need answers, Salesforce Einstein for Service serves up suggested knowledge articles in just one click, saving time and improving accuracy. Einstein for Service also eliminates manual order taking, accelerating the submission process, and reducing human error. Sales benefits from AI too by scoring opportunities and predicting which ones are likely to close fastest.

With every resolved case, Einstein automatically creates new knowledge articles. This helps Einstein improve the quality and accuracy of support for similar cases in the future. And it keeps Iron Mountain's knowledge base current without additional maintenance. Iron Mountain uses the Einstein 1 Platform to get the right data, generating the right responses from AI, fully integrated into their service workflows directly into Service Cloud.

> "We've really used AI to power tremendous efficiency in case management across a high volume of cases across phone, email and chat. Due to automation routing, chat abandonment rates, for example decreased by 70%. This partnership with Salesforce and the Einstein 1 Platform is paving the way for us to redefine excellence in service."
> —*Ashish Gupta, Iron Mountain, Global Head of Client Servicing and Service Transformation*

SALESFORCE DATA CLOUD ADAPTS TO UNSTRUCTURED DATA

To expand our example of Salesforce Data Cloud, as it evolved from a marketing-centric CDP into a Customer 360 platform, it enlarged support for unstructured data and GenAI-related tooling.

Vector database: A vector database allows customers to index and perform data processing on unstructured data brought into Data Cloud from sources such as knowledge bases, sales calls, field notes, etc. Those data are curated alongside metadata and the trust layer mediating GenAI. Customer insights can be drawn from unstructured data that might previously have been very difficult or impossible to analyze.

Copilot Search: Copilot Search brings together data retrieval using semantic search. Semantic search allows users to search the underlying data by meaning and context rather than keywords. The mechanism behind both vector databases and semantic search is called *vector embedding*, an ML subdiscipline. Embeddings can be thought of as a series of numbers or coordinates that index where data such as text and images are cataloged. Objects with similar characteristics are grouped together in so-called vector space. These proximate spaces allow the machine to identify content with similar intentions, even if they don't share exactly the same words.

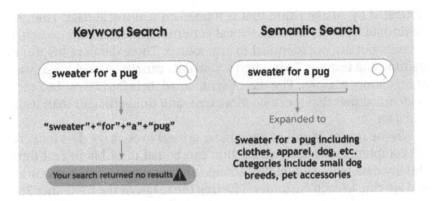

FIGURE 8.4 Example of a Keyword Search Versus a Semantic Search

Copilot Search was built with retrieval-augmented generation (RAG) to drive more trusted and relevant results. RAG allows Salesforce to pre-train models so AI can be more relevant to customers by sending the prompt augmented by data during runtime. This means the prompt is backed by semantics—the context, meaning, and intent—to improve the quality of generated outcomes compared to straightforward keywords. After passing through the trust layer, customers' LLMs are accessed to generate a response based on the augmented prompt.

Next, companies need to have the *authority* and permission to use the data. Consent is a key aspect for building trust and ethical use of data (more on this in Chapter 15). For example, a company with multiple brands, geography-specific business units, or new brands brought in via acquisition may have datasets that are subject to different consent rules. These companies need to use logic to partition data to comply.

For example, Data Cloud addresses this requirement through data spaces, which segregate data, metadata, and processes into categories. When the user brings data in from any source, they associate data lake objects (DLOs) to the relevant data space with or without filters. After the DLO mapping, they can use the data space for creating relevant data models, calculated insights, identity resolution, data insights and actions, segmentation, activation, and so on. This enables users to see and work on data specific to their domain, which is controlled by administrative permissions.

Synthetic data: In our new world of advancing AI, a new type of data has emerged called synthetic data. These data are artificially generated by an algorithm that is trained on real-world data. The synthetic data have the same statistical patterns and correlations as actual datasets but are not identical to any source. These data are helpful in training and testing LLMs when actual data cannot be used for privacy or regulatory reasons. The use of synthetic data is fairly new, but early evidence shows that it can be more cost- and time-efficient than using real data.

In the future, it will be even more critical to package data and create complete customer profiles that can be fed to LLMs in real time. Quality data will yield quality actions and responses that are accurate and specific to each customer—fueling the magic of the Customer 360.

***

CHAPTER 9

Customer Data in the Enterprise Today

Around the time Salesforce launched Service Cloud to support customer care, a technology analyst named Joe Bugajski wrote an influential paper called "Data Integration: Fantasies and Facts." In it, he warned: "Data integration is a difficult engineering process, not a product. A failed data integration program can lead to regulatory problems, incur excessive IT costs, and result in lost revenue."[1]

The author's main point remains true today: the most common data integration fantasy is that there is (or even should be) a "huge central data warehouse" that contains every piece of enterprise data "in perfect synchronicity with all business system contexts." Challenges to this pervasive vision quest are the difficulty of translating data among systems, the reality that nobody can or will take responsibility for the master store, and data regulations.

Data related to the Customer 360 exists in many enterprise systems. We've argued that some form of customer data platform is the most efficient way to realize the Data pillar of Data + AI + Trust. But what about all those other systems storing customer data? What is their role? How do they function with the CDP? In this chapter, we'll take a look at the various key systems, their evolution, and the future.

CUSTOMER RELATIONSHIP MANAGEMENT

CRM is a constellation of technologies and processes that guide and measure interactions with customers, often related to business accounts. Its purpose is to keep and convert those customers and improve metrics such as customer lifetime value (CLTV). It addresses multiple channels, including email, mobile, chat, social, and websites.

CRM emerged in the late 1980s as contact management software and—like the related CDP category, which came later—began with a focus on marketing. A discipline called database marketing arose to organize customer data and use statistical techniques to identify people most likely to respond to certain treatments. A Cambridge physicist named Robert Shaw introduced the ideas of CLTV and channel management.

Early CRM systems like TeleMagic and ACT! (which stood for Automated Contact Tracking) described themselves as a modern version of the Rolodex, a circular card file once popular for organizing names, addresses, phone numbers, as well as personal details. Gradually, these digital Rolodexes started to integrate with marketing automation tools to do more than store customer data.

An Oracle employee named Tom Siebel launched Siebel CRM in 1993 and created a bigger market; database companies, particularly those with enterprise resource planning (ERP) offerings, began to add CRM-like features into their sales, service, and ERP products. Some startups aimed at small to medium businesses also appeared. This was primarily on-premise software.

When Salesforce launched in 1999, it was an ASP, or software that was hosted for organizations on the cloud. It was not yet modern software-as-a-service but was nonetheless seen as subversive. The company itself has even admitted: "Salesforce did not create a great stir when it launched in 1999; most competitors regarded cloud services as a fad and not a good vehicle for CRM."

Over time, the CRM market settled into operational and analytical components:

- *Salesforce automation*—tools for sales professionals to track contacts, accounts, history, and conversion
- *Service automation*—support for direct customer service including phone, email, and knowledge
- *Marketing automation*—tools that support customer marketing journeys and automate tasks such as delivering messages
- *Analytics*—applying data mining, visualization, and statistical techniques to customer data for reporting and analysis

As described in *Customer Data Platforms*, when it appeared in the late 2010s, the CDP category was often confused with CRM. After all, the "C" in both categories stands for *customer*. In time, analysts realized CDP and CRM were related but have distinct domains.

The person who named the CDP category is the legendary analyst David Raab. He identified CDPs in a blog post in 2013 and founded the Customer Data Platform Institute 3 years later.[2] By 2016, the category had gone mainstream and one of your authors (Martin) was covering it as an industry analyst at Gartner, which added the CDP to its market-barometer Hype Cycle in 2016.

Presciently, Raab did not confine the CDP to marketing users in his original blog post: "The new systems [i.e., CDPs] can also feed sales, customer service, online advertising, point of sale, and any other customer-facing systems. I'll . . . hereby christen the concept as 'Customer Data Platform.'"[3] (Raab later admitted he wanted a name that would make a melodic acronym.)

So you can see that the CDP is a higher-level system[4] that uses data from the CRM ("sales, customer service"), but many other systems as well. The challenge CDPs arose to meet was that customer data were hard to move around, requiring APIs and manual pipelines. Another challenge was that different vendors' applications using customer data did not work very well together.

As we've said, the CDP was designed to free trapped data.

MASTER DATA MANAGEMENT

Master data management (MDM) deals with master data—obviously—which is basically just data that are important to the business about entities such as people (e.g., customers, suppliers), places (stores, offices), and things (products, etc.). MDM is a rigorous, highly controlled set of tools and processes to describe and manage all this data—but it isn't the data itself.

MDM focuses on operational data rather than transactional data (orders, receipts). So it's often treating the same information that's in the CRM and the CDP. Think of it as a way to organize the company's data so that any particular piece has a lineage, hierarchy, and place; it's supposed to be foundational and stable, professionalizing the "core data" the organization needs to succeed.

Part of the purpose of MDM is to provide a common definition for important entities like a "Customer," one that will hold across business units and regions. It aims to standardize different policies and clean up departmental idiosyncrasies, which can be rampant.

In general, MDM covers three major domains:

- Customers
- Products
- Locations

It ties all records, copies, and changes back to the core master data, so MDM is supposed to provide a reliable way to have a "single source of truth" for important data. Remember that MDM is really just an index and a set of definitions that organize and link data. The data itself can be stored in different ways but are often in a master data repository like an enterprise data warehouse.

MDM arose in the 1990s as enterprise data proliferated, and it was widely adopted in part to support regulatory requirements like the Sarbanes-Oxley Act and the European Union's Solvency II Directive, which require strict auditability of data. So in addition to being a technology, MDM encompasses processes and people, defining data owners and stewards, governance, schemas, and taxonomies.

As you can see, MDM is a major undertaking and can be expensive. Most enterprises have some version in place; success levels vary. As a set of definitions and processes, it cannot replace CRM or CDP but will definitely be needed to inform their implementation.

ENTERPRISE DATA WAREHOUSES

There has always been creative tension among IT, so-called shadow IT, and the business user. In the 1970s, the introduction of 4GL technology popularized the idea that computer programming and software systems should be easy enough not to require a PhD to decipher; ordinary people should be able to do things themselves, without waiting for experts.

This is true, but democratization can create problems. Different business units began to maintain their own data sources, which meant there was often redundancy and inconsistency across the enterprise. Data needed to be treated as more of an asset, and made more reliable, so vendors like IBM and Teradata developed the idea of a data warehouse.

These warehouses stored data in structured relational databases, and the data were accessed using Structured Query Language (SQL), which is still standard. Once companies began using personal computers and laptops and plugged into the internet, the data disorganization problem got worse. So version 2.0 of the data warehouse was championed by William Inmon, among others.

Inmon defined the four main characteristics of this new enterprise data warehouse (EDW) as follows:

1. Organized by "subject," or business domain (sales, service, etc.)
2. Consistency among data formats
3. Remains stable (read-only) and stored for years
4. Includes time stamps for auditing and tracking changes

There were always ways to architect an EDW, different configurations and layouts for storage, staging, connections, sandboxes, and so on. Like MDM, EDWs are still very much with us, but they in turn present challenges to the modern enterprise:

- EDWs support the stability of data but not real-time analysis and triggers.
- They can require extensive overhead and governance.
- They tend to rely on extract-transform-load (ETL) processes to move data.

The latter can be a fraught activity. It involves reformatting, copying, and moving data in a way that is supposed to be consistent, but the process can also be overly rigid and time-consuming. Later improvements include extract-load-transform (ELT), where the raw data are stored in the EDW and transformed when needed for use.

> "[ETL is] the bane of every data scientist and team as they try to get data into shape and put it to work."
>
> —*TechCrunch*

More recent improvements include the development of the logical data warehouse, data federation, and virtualization. These technologies provide a way to make use of data without physically transforming it, copying, or moving it from one place to another. Transformation and transport take time and computational resources and introduce error and data-synchronization risks.

Data lakes: As we have seen, data lakes appeared in the big data era, when companies were overwhelmed with data from internet-connected computers, mobile devices, sensors, social networks, digital ads, IoT, and more. A data lake supports massive data storage in its original format (no ETL or relational requirements). Data are accessed using so-called NoSQL methods (not-only-SQL, meaning SQL is not required but can be used) when it is needed.

Homegrown data lakes can be difficult to use. They also encourage data dumping; users can be like hoarders who have closets full of stuff they "might need someday" but really don't. Gartner famously said that 90% of the data stored in most data lakes would never be used and that they threatened to become data swamps. Some data lake users simply continued the wishful thinking of an earlier generation of data warehouses users.

> "For years and years and years, everybody tried to put everything in one place with the data warehouse, and that didn't work. Well, it doesn't work with a data lake, either."
> —*Donald Feinberg, Gartner*

Data marts: Domain-specific data marts arose as a kind of more narrowly scoped data lake with a subset of data relevant to a particular domain. For example, Land O'Lakes built a data mart that contained campaign-level data for all its marketing channels, including social networks and advertising, and used this to power a continually updated control panel displaying company results across its brands.

Data lake houses: As we mentioned in the context of Salesforce Data Cloud, a data lake house architecture combines elements of the data warehouse and the data lake. Bill Inmon himself called the data lakehouse an "extension or evolution of the data warehouse," with additional support for more data types, including unstructured text.

MODERN DATA WAREHOUSE (SNOWFLAKE)

Around 2012, somewhere in San Mateo, California, a trio of refugees from Oracle and other database vendors decided to build a new data warehouse. Rather than adapting it to the cloud, it would be designed from the ground-up specifically for cloud environments. It would be agnostic across ecosystems like Amazon, Google, and Microsoft. It would reduce a lot of the mouse-breaking administrative overhead required for hardware and software configuration. Ultimately, it would democratize access to data for analytics.

Emerging from stealth mode in 2015, Snowflake rolled out another refulgent innovation: it separated storage and compute. Storage is where data sit, and compute is the layer that does something to that data: calculations, updates, transformations. EDWs linked storage and compute together, since it was more efficient to do computations close to the data. Infrastructure improvements made it possible for Snowflake to separate these processes.

This separation brings advantages. Since both storage and compute cost money, users can scale one element up (or down) without impacting the cost of the other. Multiple compute nodes can be applied at the same time to the same data without slowing anyone down, so users with different requirements have more flexibility. It eliminated the need for customers to have different storage for functional areas like business intelligence and marketing—users could write different queries on the same data, at the same time. Meanwhile, Snowflake automatically handled tasks like data distribution, partitioning, and optimizations.

Snowflake became popular quickly and is a market leader today. It introduced further innovations like the ability to load data in real time and real-time monitoring (Snowpipe). A data marketplace was launched in 2020, and like Salesforce before it, Snowflake opened access to the platform for developers to write and execute custom code (Snowpark).

Data sharing: But the innovation most relevant to our Customer 360 discussion was Snowflake Data Sharing. First rolled out in 2017, it allowed users to share data objects among different accounts without moving or copying them. Users didn't even have to be Snowflake customers; outsiders could set up a "reader account" and participate in data sharing. It's a very useful feature: the data analyst and blogger Rick Van Der Lans likens it to streaming movies or music—data on demand.

Data sharing without copying or moving is often called zero-ETL or zero-copy. It is now embraced by many vendors in addition to Snowflake. An example is Amazon Aurora, often used as a system for large volumes of online transactional data. It offers a zero-ETL integration with Amazon Redshift, a data warehouse often used for analytics and reporting.

Some leading CDPs find zero-ETL integrations with cloud warehouses like Snowflake, Databricks, and Google's BigQuery very useful. Companies will often store data in Snowflake that is not directly about customers but might be relevant to the Customer 360. For example, vehicle maintenance information can be essential to providing better service for an insurance customer, supply-chain data can improve product recommendations, and so on.

Data clean rooms: In recent years, data clean rooms (DCRs) have emerged as a way for different parties to share data without providing access to raw data. The first commercial clean rooms were introduced by Facebook and Google for their advertising customers, who could use their own first-party data to try to find their customers among Facebook's and Google's users for ad targeting and measurement. (Match rates were usually high.) These customers would never see raw Facebook or Google or data, but the "clean room" was a strictly controlled, privacy-safe environment to allow data sharing.

Additional types of DCRs emerged, including standalone platforms and startups built using Snowflake's data sharing features. To our knowledge, no CDP also offers a full-featured DCR—and this makes sense. DCRs are a purpose-built technology that stresses privacy; they work best as highly separated, high-trust environments. (We talk more about collaboration technologies in Chapter 14.)

CDPs and data warehouses: Some data practitioners wonder why they'd need a CDP if they already have a data warehouse like Snowflake, particularly if that warehouse contains a lot of customer data. CDPs vary in scope, but the best of them provide capabilities not designed into data warehouses; they are a tool designed to unlock data for a Customer 360.

Some considerations on this point:

- Some data may not have landed in the warehouse (e.g., streaming data).
- A CDP likely has functional capabilities not in the warehouse, like change detection, triggered actions, identity management, aggregated calculated metrics, advanced segmentation, and AI.

- Some data warehouse capabilities may require advanced skills to use; they're not available to business users.
- If the CDP has a platform ecosystem, it's easier and faster to connect to its apps, features, and partners.

FINAL CONSIDERATIONS

In 2024, the analyst firm Winterberry released a report on the state of data in the enterprise. As part of that report, they presented the conceptual visualization of analytical systems related to what we call Customer 360, shown in Figure 9.1.

Themes uncovered in the report include the rising importance of first-party data; the CDP's transition to more real-time decisions; the use

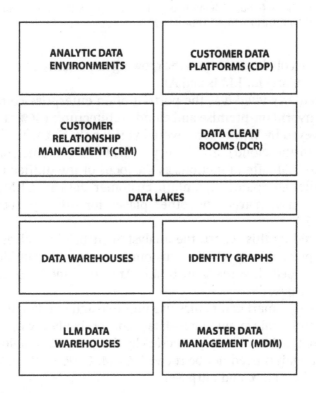

FIGURE 9.1 Customer Data Domains

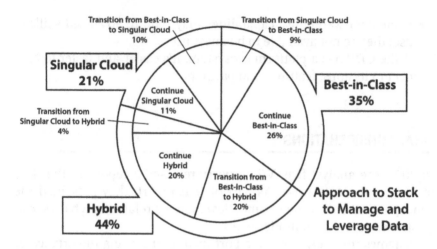

FIGURE 9.2 Approaches to Customer Data Stack (%)
Source: Winterberry Group, "Demystifying the Data Layer: The Transformation of Marketing Data Infrastructure," February 2024.

of DCRs for collaboration; and the growing importance of unstructured data, particularly for LLMs and AI.

Particularly vivid was the portrait of an enterprise composed of hybrids: hybrid on-premise and cloud architectures (56% of respondents surveyed by Winterberry were hybrid; only 12% were fully transitioned to the cloud), and a very hybridized customer data story. While the CDP often functions as the locus of the unified Customer 360 profile, companies maintain customer data in CRMs, EDWs, data lakes and marts, and other places for other purposes. (See Figure 9.2.)

Inspired by this report, the analyst Scott Brinker released a provocative piece asking whether customer data can be "unified, federated, and siloed all at the same time?" And concluded: "Yes, and each serves a purpose."[5]

In reality, smart companies use multiple and overlapping systems to store and analyze customer data—and probably always will. The EDW and data lake "fantasy" decried by the analysts Donald Feinberg and Joe Bugajski need not be revived. CRM, CDP, EDW, data lakes—each has their place and purpose.

"While some architectural purists may object," says Brinker, "I think this [hybrid approach] can be a pragmatic design pattern."

Ultimately, data can't be divorced from their context, including the applications and business purposes they serve. The Customer 360 requires accurate, available, updated customer data derived from a number of different sources. The CDP is often the best way to rise to this challenge.

***

Composable Versus Packaged and Build Versus Buy

There was a time when a kid who wanted to play with a toy building actually had to buy a toy building. Then a Danish woodworker named Ole Kirk Christiansen invented the Lego brick. Suddenly, there was almost no limit to what could be put together from this simple building block.

In a sense, the same thing happened in software design. Over the past few decades, the computer programs we use have been "broken down" into components called services and microservices that can be assembled—Lego-style —into a wide range of different solutions.

The result is a world where technically advanced Customer 360 professionals and their IT colleagues can think about building a lot of things themselves that would have been too difficult in the past. Combined with the power of open-source software and cloud providers like Amazon and Google, the new Lego mentality makes do-it-yourself (DIY) tempting.

But is it right for your own approach to improving the customer experience? Should you avoid packaged software, strap on the tool belt, and go all DIY on your stack? The answer depends on your tolerance for risk, your team's technical expertise, your timeline, and an understanding of the trade-offs involved.

DO-IT-YOURSELF OR DO-IT-FOR-ME?

What we're calling Lego-brick software has a number of more technical family names, of course: API-driven, headless, and componentized. These are not synonymous, but all point to architectures that assemble larger structures from smaller, more self-contained components. One of the more popular buzzwords recently is "composable," which is being spread around by some software vendors like chum off a shark boat.

In particular—and relevant to our Customer 360 data pillar discussion—the so-called "composable CDP" is a phenomenon that puzzles a lot of CX technology buyers. What does it mean? Is a composable CDP truly a new invention, just clever marketing, or something in between?

Currently, you've got two major CDP options to help you store and organize your customer data: full featured or composable. What's the difference? Adopting a full-featured CDP is like having furniture delivered to your home; a composable CDP is more like packing up the family and heading out to IKEA. In the latter case, assembly is required.

You can use full-featured CDPs to access data from key sources, harmonize it, manage identity, and build and activate audiences for marketing, service, and more. Composable solutions claim to provide a flexible architecture that can be adapted to your business requirements.

"If you think good architecture is expensive, try bad architecture."
—Brian Foote, developer

The good news is that you can combine the benefits of full-featured CDPs and composability without compromising on features or flexibility. For example, you can maintain a modern cloud data warehouse and still have push-button access to CRM data, as well as all the features you require for CDP use cases, without having to select and maintain a portfolio of applications.

How can you do this? Short answer: adopt a full-featured CDP that has composable benefits like modularity. Longer answer: in this chapter, we'll review what composability offers and the requirements for a full-featured CDP; then, we'll talk about how to get the best of both.

But first, let's define what a composable CDP is and how it differs from a full-featured CDP.

WHAT IS A COMPOSABLE CDP, AND HOW DOES IT WORK?

A composable CDP runs on a data warehouse and requires users to assemble the features they would like to include, much like building blocks. Components that this type of CDP probably does not offer natively (such as advanced identity management) can be supplied by other vendors. It is common for composable CDPs to have multiple vendors coexisting in the end solution, each performing different functions.

Composability is a concept in software design, and it's widely used. For example, Wix helps customers build websites from different pieces—that's composable. Data scientists rely on packaged libraries of functions that plug into Python and R—that's composable. When thinking about a composable CDP versus a full-featured CDP, it's important to keep in mind that composability is an architecture, not a product.

What does composability mean for CDPs? To gain the benefits of composability, you need to look for a CDP that's built using an architectural approach that supports modularity. It needs to be flexible, with robust application programming interfaces (APIs), and a lot of options for configuration and use case support.

The advantage of a full-featured CDP built using composable principles is it gives customers a wider range of options for implementation and deployment. For example, we know customers of Salesforce Data Cloud who do their own identity management in a homegrown solution, relying on the CDP for segmentation and activation.

The same kind of modularity helps customers who want to do their own segmentation and audience building, say, rather than use the CDP's built-in tools.

WHAT IS A FULL-FEATURED CDP, AND HOW DOES IT WORK?

A full-featured CDP is a tool designed to organize customer data from different sources and provide an up-to-date, unified view of each customer. Unlike composable CDPs, full-featured CDPs contain all the CDP capabilities in a single product, including data ingestion, modeling, identity management, and segmentation.

As detailed in our book, *Customer Data Platforms*, full-featured CDPs arose to fill a need in the market: combining disparate data to create a connected customer experience across marketing, service, sales, commerce, and beyond. They also provide a necessary foundation for AI and GenAI applications.

That's why there's so much investment and innovation in the full-featured (also known as packaged) CDP sector. According to the analyst firm IDC, the packaged CDP market is expected to surpass $5.7 billion in 2026, growing about 18% per year.[1]

As is natural in a fast-moving sector, misconceptions arise. We are happy to report they are nothing to worry about:

- Full-featured CDPs are not "legacy" systems.
- They do not create another customer data silo.

Full-featured CDPs are far from being last generation's technology. On the contrary, the best full-featured CDPs are built using cloud architectures that avoid the challenges of legacy databases, both in speed and data requirements.

And saying that CDPs create yet another silo is kind of like saying the Google search engine creates just another website. Rather, full-featured CDPs take siloed data and make them available to the business. It's the key to your customer data, not the lock. And as we've seen, some full-featured CDPs provide access to data in data warehouses like Snowflake without copying.

FULL-FEATURED OR COMPOSABLE CDP: WHICH IS BETTER FOR CUSTOMER EXPERIENCE?

Full-featured CDPs, unlike composable CDPs, have certain capabilities that make them foundational for a more connected customer experience or Customer 360. We saw this with Formula 1. When the global racing and entertainment company needed to develop profiles of its 500 million fans around the world and connect with customers across channels like mobile, the web, and advertising, the company required all the features of a Customer 360 platform.

Full-featured CDPs are designed to do at least five things:

1. Access data easily from sources like websites and warehouses.
2. Harmonize the data so they are consistent.
3. Handle identity management.
4. Create and explore segments and audiences.
5. Activate audiences to channels like email, advertising, call centers, etc.

Which brings us to a challenge of composability: it's not a set of features. So we always recommend that any technology buyer be absolutely sure that any product calling itself a composable CDP can do all the things that a good CDP does. That's just common sense.

Companies that decide to go the do-it-yourself composable CDP route often find themselves taking on more technical overhead than they anticipated. They may have to implement and manage multiple tools from multiple vendors, without a common user interface or service-level agreements. The requirements for ongoing maintenance can be significant.

Another characteristic of full-featured CDPs is that they are generally designed to be business user-friendly, using clicks, not code. This distinguishes them from legacy tools and some warehouses that require a more technical user, raising talent and training costs.

CAN A FULL-FEATURED CDP BE COMPOSABLE?

Luckily, a requirement of full-featured CDPs is *not* that you have to settle for a partial solution. It is possible to work with a CDP that's also composable in principle—that combines a full CDP feature set with the added flexibility of a composable architecture.

One way to think about the different types of CDPs is to compare their approaches to standard CDP capabilities, such as data ingestion and analytics. In general, cloud warehouses and vendors of so-called reverse-ETLs target a more technical, do-it-yourself user.

	Advanced Enterprise CDP	Cloud Warehouse
Access to CRM data	Easy point-and-click direct access to objects in CRM	Requires connector
CRM access to CDP data	Direct zero-copy access to data in CDP from CRM	Requires connector
Access to data warehouse	Direct zero-copy access or file transfer	Usually included
Ingest from other apps	App marketplace, APIs, transfer	Marketplace, connectors, or custom

(continued)

(continued)

	Advanced Enterprise CDP	Cloud Warehouse
Identity resolution	Advanced probabilistic capabilities built in	Basic features or via partners
Identity graph	Unify any customer or entity data (e.g., events, model scores, attributes)	Managed in data warehouse
Schema used	Flexible, fully customizable schema	None
Storage	Can support multi-substrate cloud	Multi-cloud
Analytics	Point-and-click, native, and BYOM*	SQL based
Data activation	Marketplace, direct to destination, or via transfer	From data warehouse
Cost	Consumption based; pay for what you use	Pay for features
Compliance	Often GDPR, CCPA, and HIPAA compliant	May require BAA for HIPAA compliance
User personas	Designed for personas from the business user (no code) to developers (pro code)	Targets technical users (pro code)

*Bring-your-own-model, such as Amazon Sagemaker

Of course, there's more to composability than just the CDP. Profile data should sit within the context of an enterprise architecture that enables you to build a more connected customer experience across your entire enterprise—from advertising through conversion, loyalty, service, winback, and more.

This more ambitious approach requires real flexibility at the platform level. So it makes a lot of sense to ensure any full-featured CDP you're considering has the flexibility and modularity advantages that you might find in a composable CDP.

It also makes sense to scrutinize any product—whether it's called "composable" or not—to make sure it's going to do what you need it to do. In the case of CDPs, your requirements likely include data access, identity management, analytical workflows, and activation.

HOW CAN A CDP COMPLEMENT YOUR DATA WAREHOUSE?

One of the key claims of both "composable CDP" and reverse-ETL vendors is that they provide zero-copy or zero-ETL access to data in cloud data warehouses like Snowflake. But as we mentioned in the Introduction, the zero-copy paradigm is a built-in feature of the best data warehouses themselves and is already available in some leading full-featured CDPs.

Since this technology levels a key distinction among composable and full-featured CDPs, we'll spend a moment describing how it works and why it's such a shift from other methods of handling customer data.

Remember the last time you moved? You probably had to pack up too much stuff, transport it in a truck, and unpack it in the new location—hoping it survived the trip. Now imagine I told you that you didn't have to move anything—your furniture could just appear in the new place in perfect condition. Well, it's not true in the physical world, but exactly that scenario is now possible with your customer data.

Thanks to technology we'll call zero-ETL, it is possible to share data among two or more data stores without actually moving it. This practice is welcome news to companies that store data in a cloud data warehouse like Snowflake or Google BigQuery. Some of them are even reluctant to adopt a CDP as part of their Customer 360 architecture because they don't want to "duplicate" data.

They don't have to. Using zero-ETL technology, users can get the benefits of a CDP—like data harmonization, identity management, built-in analytics, and activation—without the downside of physical data movement.

How does zero-ETL work? What are its benefits?

ZERO-ETL IS NOT YOUR UNCLE'S COPY AND PASTE

Copying data from one database to another is a common practice. Often, this process entails some form of data transformation, typically ETL. It can be a useful and even necessary step in managing enterprise data.

But it has its challenges. The following table highlights some of the differences between traditional (copying) methods and the zero-ETL approach.

	Traditional	Zero-ETL
Replication	Source data copied from original location to target.	Data remain in original location.
Updates	Data only accurate as of last synchronization point.	Data are accessed in real time.
Cost	User pays cost of moving and synching data.	No data movement cost.
Regulatory Requirements	Harder to keep up with compliance due to more complex governance.	User only responsible for source data.
Errors	Any data movement introduces potential for errors or mistakes.	No movement errors.
Complexity	Copying and synching creates more complexity.	Easier to manage.

Typically, the physical copying of data incurs costs for data transportation, introduces the potential for errors, complicates data governance and management, and creates data-synching time lags.

So how does zero-ETL work? The actual mechanism differs from platform to platform and is different whether you are accessing data from the CDP into the data warehouse or vice versa. In the following examples, for convenience, we'll be using Salesforce Data Cloud as the CDP and its partner Snowflake as the data warehouse. Other vendors could be substituted without significantly changing the explanation.

HOW IT WORKS: FROM CDP TO DATA WAREHOUSE

In this case, we are inside our data warehouse and want to access data that is in the CDP. In other words, information is going *out* from the CDP to the data warehouse. This process is sometimes called *data sharing*.

Data sharing usually goes through the following steps:

1. Identify the objects—or data structures—within the CDP you'd like to share. In the case of Data Cloud, these are called Data Lake Objects (cleansed data), Data Model Objects (structured by the CDP user for their business cases), and Calculated Insights Objects (for formulas like lifetime value).
2. Using point-and-click, link these objects to the data share target, in this case Snowflake.
3. Inside Snowflake, the user can perform queries across data in Snowflake as well as the objects linked via the data share—all at the same time.

Behind the scenes, the process creates "virtual tables" that describe the Data Cloud data to Snowflake. A virtual table is like a window into data in a database, but instead of copying and storing actual data, a virtual table only contains the *structure* of the data. It's a blueprint or pointer to the right place in the CDP to get the data—but the data itself stays in the CDP.

HOW IT WORKS: FROM DATA WAREHOUSE TO CDP

Now we are inside our CDP and would like to access data that are sitting in our data warehouse. This process is sometimes referred to as *data federation*.

There are many good reasons to do this. Data warehouses like Snowflake and BigQuery usually contain a massive amount of data, including transactional data like purchases, and product data. Although not typical "customer" data, such information can be very useful when trying to calculate a customer's loyalty status or build a recommendation based on details about products they buy.

The steps to access warehouse data in the CDP are as follows:

1. Salesforce Data Cloud mounts tables from the data warehouse as external data lake objects. (Mounting is a process that creates a virtual data blueprint, like the one described previously.)
2. Data Cloud performs its usual functions such as ID management, analysis, segmentation, etc.

3. The CDP can access data from the data warehouse by performing federated (or combined) queries that include data in Data Cloud and the objects that are provided by the data warehouse.

ZERO-ETL/ZERO-COPY IN REAL LIFE

The success of cloud-native data warehouses like Snowflake, Databricks, BigQuery, and Amazon Redshift makes a lot of sense. Most larger enterprises have at least experimented with them, and many use them as an integral part of their data architectures.

But no data warehouse performs the functions of a CDP like Salesforce Data Cloud or other market leaders. Key CDP functions include identity management, user-friendly analytics and segmentation, and—most important—a portfolio of options to use what is learned in the CDP, from advertising to messaging (e.g., email, SMS, WhatsApp) to call-center experiences and e-commerce recommendations.

Delivery company: For example, imagine a delivery company wanted to build a unified customer profile in a CDP while being able to access many petabytes of shopping data stored in a data warehouse. This on-demand delivery service wanted to improve the performance of its premium subscription service.

The company implemented a CDP to provide a single view of its customers in hundreds of cities across the United States and Canada. To supplement the data in the CDP, it also needed to access some of the millions of customer orders it processes yearly, housed in Snowflake.

Using the zero-ETL connection between the CDP and Snowflake, the company has access to the purchase data it needs to build predictive models, ultimately to deliver better offers, messages, and experiences to its subscription members.

Recall that larger enterprises can have an average of 976 different applications running the businesses, according to a report by data integration company MuleSoft. Meanwhile the amount of data created, captured, copied, and consumed is expected to more than double by 2026, according to IDC.[2] Thanks to the power of zero-ETL data sharing, the looming explosion of Customer 360–related data will be easier to manage.

***

CHAPTER 11

What Does "Real Time" Really Mean?

Not long ago, a global study of customer experience professionals uncovered a paradox. Respondents regularly ranked "Engaging with customers in real time" as one of their most important strategic priorities . . . and also, poignantly, as one of their greatest challenges. In previous years, real-time engagement was the number one challenge.

What does this say about overworked Customer 360 technologists?

We think there is a lot of confusion about exactly what *real-time customer engagement* means. Even a casual web search reveals a potpourri of inconsistent definitions. One seemingly reliable source says it's "systematically responding to your customer," while another—no less authoritative—defines it as "focusing on . . . customer feedback." Certainly, both are important. But are they enough?

Newer technologies, including CDPs and data warehouses, are putting more real-time data into the hands of practitioners, who can use it to improve their service, chatbots, product recommendations, campaigns, analytics, and so on. While it's important to capture and process data rapidly, it's not always necessary to act on it right away. Real time does not have to mean right now—and often, an immediate response is exactly the wrong thing to do for your Customer 360.

We're not denying that faster is usually better than slower. But there is always a foundational trade-off between the overhead (storage, compute, configuration, skills) required for instant data access and the needs of the business. To allude to a recent movie for which

Michelle Yeoh won a well-deserved Academy Award for playing an overwhelmed entrepreneur, is having *Everything Everywhere All at Once* always the most efficient way to work?

The answer is . . . *probably not.*

WHAT DO WE MEAN BY "REAL TIME"?

Most of the time, when we say "real time," what we really mean is "right time." It's delivering the right data at the right moment, to the right systems, to maximize our moments with the customer. It's about having a ranked set of recommendations available when a customer appears on the website or engages with a bot. It's about customizing the experience on an in-store kiosk or an in-car screen based on what the person seems to want to do. It's about not making someone re-enter information into an app that they just told an agent at the counter.

However, it doesn't necessarily follow that nailing the "right-time" experience requires that all your customer data be available instantly, everywhere. This is actually good news. Any real-time data ubiquity requirement is not only technically unrealistic, but it also imposes a heavy burden on technical and human resources, not to mention partners.

- Right time—doing what is needed to make each moment count for the customer
- Real time—collecting and processing data with no delay

The reason to make this distinction is that there is a technical and organizational cost to imposing real-time requirements on customer experience teams. Some teams have resources to handle it; some don't. In the current climate, it's more important to make strategic investments into the systems that need to be real time—like the CDP—and understand what's required elsewhere.

> "While brands may need constant access to bi-directional data for real-time personalization, large batch data uploads may better suit data not updated or leveraged in real-time."
> —*Winterberry Group, "Demystifying the Data Layer"*

AN EXAMPLE: A WELL-KNOWN AIRLINE

The travel and hospitality industry is one of the world's most sensitive to the dimension of time. If a customer's digital profile is not accurate in the moment, some very unfortunate events can occur: flights are missed, seats aren't changed, complaints fly around on social networks.

When a customer makes a change to their seat or flight on the airline's app or website, they expect it to show up in their experience right away. So when they go to a kiosk or a service counter, or call customer care, they assume—very reasonably, of course—that the screen or person (via their own screen) knows what they did. Customers also likely assume the airline won't send them irrelevant emails or offers, will alert them to important changes like gates and ETDs, and otherwise respect the realities of modern journeying.

Leading airlines have spent millions of dollars in recent years ensuring their critical operational systems can support real-time information at scale. But this example also demonstrates the difference between real-time data and a specific Customer 360 use case like marketing. Real-time operational systems should update the customer's profile right away. On the other hand, marketing should happen at *whatever speed is right for the customer*—whether that's today, in 5 minutes, or next week.

Bear in mind that there can be a very significant—sometimes multimillion dollar—difference between supporting sub-millisecond (real-time) responses versus sub-minute (near real time) or slightly longer responses. When customers are on the website or app, they likely expect their actions to be processed in milliseconds (under a second). But there's no reason the call center can't be updated in a few seconds and email in a minute or so, right?

Lowering absolute response rates can lower costs and complexity without impacting the customer's experience at all.

DIFFERENT SPEEDS FOR DIFFERENT NEEDS

Delivering in right-time requires a strategic calculus of what the customer expects and a behind-the-scenes balance among systems, resources, and goals. How can you figure out where to draw those data-driven lines, knowing when and where you need to get something done in milliseconds, seconds, minutes, or more?

Customer experience has two basic modes:

- *Respond:* You're reacting to customers when they're already engaged. They're on your website, in your app, poking around on a kiosk in your store or dealership, or interacting with your chatbot or rep.
- *Inspire:* You're trying to get the attention of customers (and prospects) when they may not be thinking about you. You send emails with offers, show ads on social networks, or do advanced analytical modeling on their data in order to improve personalization next time you see them.

In most cases, it's the "Respond" mode that needs you to ingest, process, and activate signals from the customer in sub-second time. On the other hand, most "Inspire" activities, including modeling and AI, are preplanned and not real time. In fact, they benefit from more complete, cleansed, and curated customer data that really needs to be done *right* rather than *right now*.

In some cases, real-time responses can even be counterproductive to the Customer 360. Take an abandoned-cart email. Not many of us would react well to a reminder email—or, even worse, a text message—a mere few milliseconds after we decided to leave.

In general, a hierarchy of types of customer experiences and response times include the following:

- *Real time*—in-session personalization (website, apps, kiosks), next-best-experience within a session
- *Near real time*—call-center profiles, governance and privacy updates, triggers for journeys
- *Minutes+*—planned campaigns and tests, analytics and reporting, offer and lead scoring, partner data matching, ad suppression

CUSTOMER DATA PLATFORMS

A number of leading CDPs, data warehouses and other vendors describe their real-time capabilities. What they often don't disclose is that no existing CDP or data warehouse is completely end-to-end real time from the moment of data ingestion all the way through to

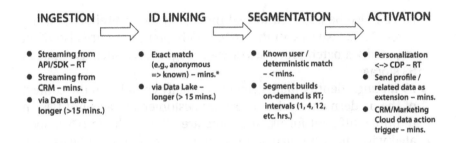

INGESTION ID LINKING SEGMENTATION ACTIVATION

- Streaming from API/SDK – RT
- Streaming from CRM – mins.
- via Data Lake – longer (>15 mins.)

- Exact match (e.g., anonymous => known) – mins.*
- via Data Lake – longer (> 15 mins.)

- Known user / deterministic match – < mins.
- Segment builds on-demand is RT; intervals (1, 4, 12, etc. hrs.)

- Personalization <-> CDP – RT
- Send profile / related data as extension – mins.
- CRM/Marketing Cloud data action trigger – mins.

DATA GRAPHS
RT ms. data layer | Built for Marketing & Sales, Service, Loyalty (entire enterprise)

FIGURE 11.1 Key Phases of Customer Data Management

the ultimate use of that data. Every system is built to support various speeds, for reasons of costs and efficiency.

A typical configuration—embraced by a number of enterprise CDPs—supports a real-time process for some streaming data, data change actions, and flows, while also having a data lake or lake house where data are located for refinement, processing, and storage. The data lake or lake house may itself support near–real time use cases, but it also uses batch and scheduled ingestion for data that doesn't require real-time treatment.

One leading CDP explicitly divides its product offering into batch and real-time versions, which work together. Most others combine the batch and real-time processes into a single data flow architecture, recognizing that most companies need both as part of their unified Customer 360 profile.

In any Customer 360 data management system, such as a CDP, data often go through a series of phases; they have what's called a life cycle (See Figure 11.1). This life cycle can be fast or slow, and each individual phase often has computational requirements that determine its speed.

As an example, the CDP often has four key phases, or processes: ingestion, identity linking (deduplication and unification), segmentation and other analytics, and activation to end points.

The four phases represent key computational moment that can take time:

- *Ingestion:* Data can stream in real time from APIs, tags, and software development kits (SDKs), or from systems with native connectors.

(It can also be accessed in real time from data warehouses using zero-ETL, as we saw in the previous chapter.) Data are also often ingested via batch processes or via a staging area such as Amazon S3 storage.

- *ID linking:* Identity management is usually complex in the context of the modern enterprise. There are customer and account IDs, in multiple different forms, and there are often multiple IDs associated with the same person or account, of different vintages, that must be reconciled. Deterministic (exact, one-to-one) matches, when the same ID is present in two different records, are usually done in real time. But more complex, probabilistic, AI-modeled or hierarchical matches can take longer.
- *Segmentation:* Often a capability built into the CDP, segmentation is the process of grouping unified profiles in various ways for activation or analytics. Segments using basic attributes and profiles that have already been ID-linked are often real time. But adding computations such as streaming data requirements, multilevel waterfalls, or complex calculations (e.g., compute LTV and include) increases latency.
- *Activation:* Activation is sending data and instructions to downstream systems, such as email, SMS, call center, CRM, loyalty, web personalization, etc. Simply synching data in a CDP profile with external tools is often done in real time. Notably, this includes real-time interaction platforms (RTIM), which handle in-session personalization in particular high-traffic channels such as websites. Often sending a segment (or audience) to another system can be time limited by that system (e.g., a segment sent to Facebook ads won't launch in real time).

Many CDPs maintain a subset of customer data in a so-called "hot store" or in-memory database. This can be called the real-time profile. The purpose of this real-time profile is to make certain frequently used or high-value data available. Often structured as a graph with key attributes, related objects, and user IDs, these profiles can be extended across federated data sources such as Snowflake and BigQuery.

Another key use for these low-latency data graphs is for AI and GenAI models. Both benefit from the inclusion of more real-time data and more context around that data, from the graph. For example, an LLM will generate more relevant, personalized messages (e.g., email, web copy, call-center scripts) if it knows not only the products a person buys but also product categories, prices, and discounts, which are related objects.

REAL-TIME DATA MANAGEMENT

We hope we've added some nuance to your understanding of the "real-time" concept. Remember: at least for the foreseeable future, there is always a trade-off among real-time customer data management, cost, and complexity.

In assessing a vendor, focus on its support for your right-time—as well as real-time—needs:

1. First-party data: Many enterprises already have a trove of first-party data in existing ecosystems, and the owner of that ecosystem likely provides better access than third parties.
2. Single layer: Where possible, it's a good idea to consolidate customer data in a single data layer across modules such as RTIM and CDP.
3. Partners: Engineered integrations with important third-party partners also helps eliminate friction in the data transfer process. For example, partners are often used for tasks such as data enrichment, media activation, and auditing. Some CDPs have deep, productized connections with Meta, Google, Amazon, the Trade Desk, Epsilon, and others for this purpose.

Ultimately, any lingering confusion about what is and isn't real time fades in importance when we pose a better question: What does the customer *really need from us right now*? That's what you need the right technology to deliver.

***

CHAPTER 12

AI in Action Today!

"It is change, continuing change, inevitable change, that is the dominant factor in society today. No sensible decision can be made any longer without taking into account not only the world as it is, but the world as it will be. . . ."

—Issac Asimov (*Asimov on Science Fiction,* 1981)

The term "artificial intelligence" (AI) was first used in the mid-1950s. Progress in its initial decades was made primarily by programmatic AI methods based on logic aimed at solving discrete areas of study. The current proliferation of generative AI (GenAI) comes from pioneering research in the 1940s, when Warren McCullough and Walter Pitts established the principles of neural networks by designing computer processing methods around the understanding of how the human brain functions.[1]

Today's prolific generative AI grew from the neural network approach spurring the potential for technological innovation to reach unprecedented levels of awareness and accessibility. Earlier, we showed that ChatGPT took 2 months to achieve 100 million users compared to the mobile phone industry's 16 years and TikTok's 9 months. Equally impressive is the pace at which AI learning has accelerated—achieving skills on par with humans in shorter and shorter time frames. (See Figure 12.1.)

Klaus Schwab, founder of the World Economic Forum and author of *The Fourth Industrial Revolution,* refers to the current step-changes as the "Cyber-physical Systems" fourth Industrial Revolution. AI in combination with big data, blockchain, IoT, gene sequencing innovations, and

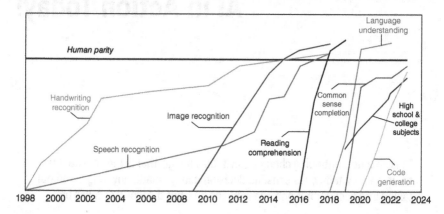

FIGURE 12.1   Time for AI Models to Reach Human Accuracy (for illustrative purposes only)
Source: "AI: The Coming Revolution," Coatue, November 16, 2023, https://www.coatue.com/blog/perspective/ai-the-coming-revolution-2023

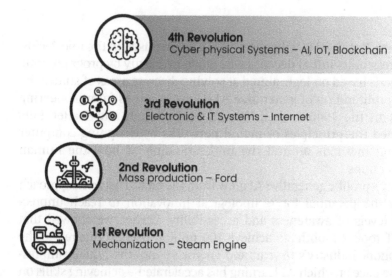

FIGURE 12.2   The Four Industrial Revolutions

other disruptive technologies—these inspire societal transformations that impact how we communicate, work, and entertain ourselves. These changes even impact our identity as individuals and across societies. (See Figure 12.2.)

One can look at these revolutions as step changes in efficiency. While the first three revolutions address mobility, production and information, the fourth solves for *human* productivity.

A BRIEF HISTORY OF AI

AI first entered mainstream conversations in 1997 when the computer program Deep Blue defeated world chess champion Garry Kasparov. Subsequently, IBM Watson won *Jeopardy!* in 2011, and the world-champion Go player was defeated by AlphaGo, a program created by Google DeepMind in 2016.[2] While AI can master complex games or mathematical equations better than perhaps the most accomplished humans in the world, it's worth noting the difficulty of creating a robot with the mobility of a 12 month old. In fact, in 1988, AI researcher Hans Moravec observed that AI can learn things that are "hard" for humans but struggle with things that are "easy" for even very young humans. This finding is now known as Moravec's paradox.[3]

Why is such marked AI acceleration happening now? Several factors have culminated to set the stage, with the first being the most critical:

- *Data:* We have 30+ years of World Wide Web data to train on. In addition, the volume of *labeled* data used in ML models has grown exponentially over the past 10 or so years.
- *Compute:* We have the GPUs and TPUs—specialized AI processor chips—to support AI workloads.
- *Architecture:* GenAI technologies have sufficiently matured, e.g., GANs, Stable Diffusion, and NerFs.[4]
- *Mass accessibility:* Natural language prompts make it relatively easy for anyone who can type to engage and use complex GenAI models such as OpenAIs.

Essentially, a nexus of conditions occurred for the GenAI rocket to take off. Since November 2022, the promise of generative AI has

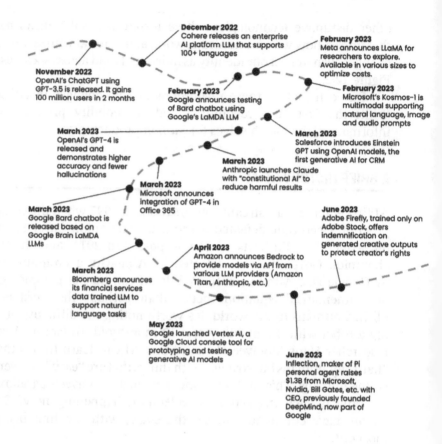

FIGURE 12.3 Recent GenAI Announcements

caught the attention of the world. There has been an ongoing frenzy of announcements and innovations from startups and the largest technology vendors in the world grabbing headlines. Many are eager to tap into this unique gold rush moment. (See Figure 12.3.)

Keeping on top of the latest news related to AI is a significant undertaking on its own. Here are just a few ways we get exposure from a variety of views on the latest news and developments:

- All In Podcast
- The AI Podcast

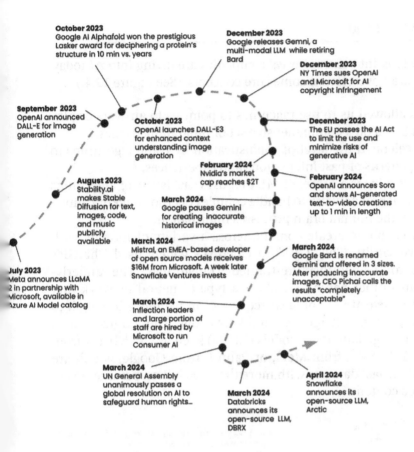

October 2023
Google AI Alphafold won the prestigious Lasker award for deciphering a protein's structure in 10 min vs. years

December 2023
Google releases Gemni, a multi-modal LLM while retiring Bard

December 2023
NY Times sues OpenAI and Microsoft for AI copyright infringement

September 2023
OpenAI announced DALL-E for image generation

October 2023
OpenAI launches DALL-E3 for enhanced context understanding image generation

December 2023
The EU passes the AI Act to limit the use and minimize risks of generative AI

August 2023
Stability.ai makes Stable Diffusion for text, images, code, and music publicly available

February 2024
Nvidia's market cap reaches $2T

February 2024
OpenAI announces Sora and shows AI-generated text-to-video creations up to 1 min in length

March 2024
Google pauses Gemini for creating inaccurate historical images

July 2023
Meta announces LLaMA 2 in partnership with Microsoft, available in Azure AI Model catalog

March 2024
Mistral, an EMEA-based developer of open source models receives $16M from Microsoft. A week later Snowflake Ventures invests

March 2024
Google Bard is renamed Gemini and offered in 3 sizes. After producing inaccurate images, CEO Pichai calls the results "completely unacceptable"

March 2024
Inflection leaders and large portion of staff are hired by Microsoft to run Consumer AI

March 2024
UN General Assembly unanimously passes a global resolution on AI to safeguard human rights...

March 2024
Databricks announces its open-source LLM, DBRX

April 2024
Snowflake announces its open-source LLM, Arctic

- The NextWavePod Podcast
- Latent Space Podcast
- Kelvin Mu on LinkedIn
- Andrew Ng on LinkedIn
- The Rundown in 5 Minutes Newsletter
- Matt Wolfe on YouTube

Consider also following some of the main VC firms investing in AI on LinkedIn, such as a16z (aka Andreessen Horowitz).

AN OVERVIEW OF AI

Before we look into current ways companies are diving into AI today, following is an overview of some core concepts. (See Figure 12.4.)

- *AI* has allowed us to use machines to point us to answers or play games based on a comprehensive set of programmed rules.
- *ML* accelerated the level of sophistication by using algorithms to study patterns of past interactions and experiences.
- *Deep Learning* is a subset of ML that uses vast layers of algorithms across a neural network to handle complex decision-making, much like how the human brain processes information.
- *GenAI* is able to create content across a variety of formats with great versatility. The "GPT" in OpenAI's widely used ChatGPT stands for Generative Pre-trained Transformer. The underlying transformer behind GenAI is a type of neural network that uses deep learning to process sequences in parallel allowing it to "learn" grammar, languages, and knowledge. These transformers draw on large language models (LLMs) such as ChatGPT-4 from OpenAI, LLaMA from Meta, or Palm-E from Google, which are trained on vast datasets with more than 100 billion parameters, to produce content.[5]

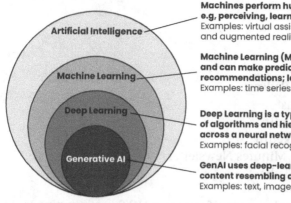

Machines perform human-like cognitive functions, e.g, perceiving, learning, reasoning
Examples: virtual assistants like Alexa or Siri, virtual and augmented reality, game-playing AI

Machine Learning (ML) algorithms detect patterns and can make predictive and prescriptive recommendations; learns from experience
Examples: time series forecasting, credit scoring

Deep Learning is a type of ML that uses vast layers of algorithms and hierarchical computing units across a neural network
Examples: facial recognition, autonomous vehicles

GenAI uses deep-learning models to generate new content resembling data on which it has trained
Examples: text, image, video, music, and code

FIGURE 12.4 Domains of AI

PREDICTIVE AND GENERATIVE AI

AI and ML that we've used for the past 20 years are often character-ized by predictive AI, which looks at past data to anticipate events or attributes in the future. It prescribes actions based on what is analyzed in existing data. GenAI creates new content based on what it has learned from existing data.

AI NEEDS HIGH OCTANE DATA AS FUEL

Examples	Predictive Informs	Generative Assists
Service	■ Customer churn predictions ■ Next best offer suggestions	■ Chatbots that manage customer service responses ■ Summarization of interaction between customer and service agent
Sales	■ Lead scoring ■ Sales forecasting	■ Account planning based on company's priorities highlighted in social media, earnings calls ■ Sales emails drawing on page context ■ Sales emails leveraging CRM data and email history
Marketing	■ Campaign response rate predictions ■ Personalized email conversion estimates	■ Subject line and email creation ■ Segment creation
Commerce	■ Pricing optimization ■ Personalized product recommendations	■ Writing product descriptions ■ Chatbot for commerce concierge
Loyalty	■ New loyalty group forecasting	■ Loyalty tier promotion messaging
General		■ Chat-based coding assistant

Evidence among enterprise AI users is that using "hybrid AI" or a combination of predictive and generative AI together is a powerful option. Here are their examples of hybrid AI use cases where generative AI helps companies to take action based on predictive AI insights (***generative*** shown in ***italics*** and **predictive** is **underlined**).

- As a marketer, I need to ***draft*** a personalized marketing email that **matches** products with propensity to buy scores
- As a business analyst, I need to ***generate*** starter code that **identifies** problem customer accounts in usage data.
- As a sales rep, I need to ***draft*** an email that is **triggered** to be sent to customers by particular criteria.
- As a service agent, I need to ***craft*** responses to customer inquiries in a way that's **informed** by company knowledge.[6]

Let's recall Moravec's Paradox: perhaps AI for language generation is the first area to thrive because of the availability of training data. The amount of text data on the internet far exceeds the data sets available on dimensions of physical space, perception, and mobility. When we look at various areas where companies can be exploring and experimenting with generative AI today, the focus is on areas where the source or the fuel—the data and models—are available and accessible.

If data are fuel, then quality data are the high octane fuel that will help you run your company to be more efficient and grow more quickly. The combination of curated data fueling AI to drive business success is a hot topic because the combination of quality data with GenAI has step-change impacts on both business efficiency and revenue potential. The stakes are going to be increasingly high within the next year to 3 years.

In our day-to-day work, we help companies to assess where they are in their digital data maturity, guided by the following chart.

If you are "beginner," you may want to invest in some turnkey ways to get your data and AI in order quickly. (See Figure 12.5.)

For those who are beginners and still designing a coordinated, comprehensive data strategy, lake house–architectured platforms such as Salesforce Data Cloud can help you curate data assets for strategic advantage. Some challenges such platforms help users to overcome are manual data collection processes, duplicate records, data silos owned by different teams, legacy systems, a fragmented data model, and a shortage of talent managing data quality.

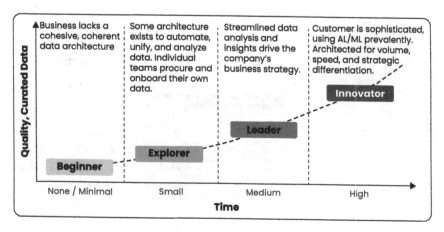

FIGURE 12.5 Data Maturity Curve

A well-structured Customer 360 platform can help unlock data that are trapped in an app, data warehouse, or other data silos. It can ingest fragmented structured and unstructured data to create a 360-degree view of customers. In the platform, customers' data are harmonized and unified with metadata to allow faster access and the ability to act on customer information across product and service interactions.

When an enterprise CDP is integrated with an AI platform, it unlocks data so they are actionable in a personalized and engaging manner across all of your Customer 360 applications, including CRM, automation, analytics, and more. Most of all, the platform becomes a trusted vault for customer data to evolve into insights. It provides the high octane fuel on which to train and ground more advanced AI. All of this occurs in the flow of work through your app experience and becomes a differentiator to better serve your customers.

For those that may be "explorers," further along the maturity curve, you may have an enterprise grade data strategy in place or under development with a data warehouse or data lake vendor. Because Customer 360 platforms like Data Cloud are designed with open and extensible architectures, they complement these investments and consolidate actionable customer data in a focused manner. This is critical in AI model development because you don't want to train your LLMs on a data dumpster filled with everything in the company. This is costly and energy intensive. You want to train on the data that drives better

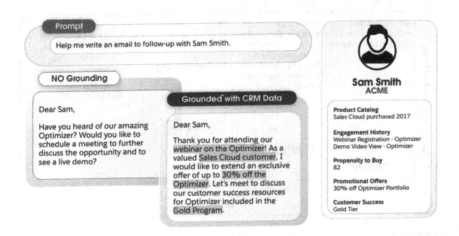

FIGURE 12.6   Improving Prompts with First-Party Data

customer experiences and insights, data that will be efficient, meaningful, and differentiating for you in your market.

GenAI can augment many key insights—and bring them to life through directed action—when AI is built into the flow of work across applications. Following is an example of a natural language prompt in a CRM that was improved using context and personalization, having trained on a company's own first-party data. (See Figure 12.6.)

Ultimately the goal of customer data is to create valuable channels of conversation. The businesses metrics with GenAI will still be tied to acquiring, retaining, and growing relationships with customers. Companies have to thread the needle of not over-reaching and being opted out, but remaining assertive enough to stay top of mind, credible, and trustworthy.

WILL GENERATIVE AI HAVE AN IMPACT ON BUSINESSES RIGHT AWAY?

The short answer is yes. But the big game-changing market acceleration is probably another year to 3 years out. What will that look like? We're expecting businesses that are AI-enabled will be able to move more quickly in their markets to grow, cut costs, and achieve higher profits. We expect most non–AI related strategic initiatives to diminish in importance. We also expect to see some detrimental mistakes too. Unbridled AI is not the answer we're recommending either because consumers have only so much tolerance for breach of trust or confidence. "Blaming the AI" won't be a credible response when the stakes are high.

Early users are seeing truly impressive speed and efficiency gains due to AI. But recall that we are just at the beginning of the journey; there is more to learn ahead. Goldman Sachs predicted in 2023 that private investments in AI—many at a seed stage—would reach $160 billion by 2025.[7] In other words, a great deal more innovation is on the horizon.

Where to start. We recommend customers start experimenting with various types and combinations of AI specifically where it can augment existing workflows with summarization, forecasting, and classification. For each potential use case, there are probably ways to use predictive (or traditional AI), generative, or a combination of predictive and generative AI. (See Figure 12.7.)

Questions may arise around using pre-trained models versus training models on your own data. Training on your own data will allow

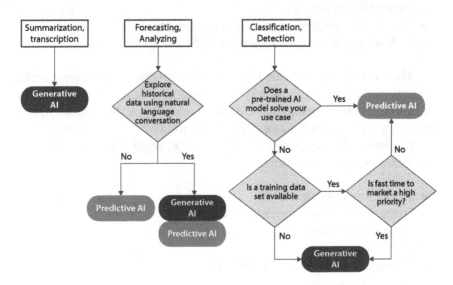

FIGURE 12.7 Use Case–Driven AI Approaches
Source: https://developers.google.com/machine-learning/problem-framing/ml-framing#identify_the_output_you_need

AI to generate content in line with your brand tone of voice and your customer relationship history. The degree of real-time personalization generative AI offers is significant as long as the Customer 360 team has its curated data unified, harmonized, and orchestrated to serve as high octane fuel. Most likely business leaders will have an ensemble or orchestra of AI models to work with and how you choose to "conduct" the various instruments will become a strategic differentiator.

HOW PREVALENT IS GenAI USE TODAY?

In a McKinsey Global Survey on AI recently, roughly, a third of respondents said they were regularly using GenAI.[8]

The percentage of respondents who reported using GenAI either at work or outside of work, by industry, were as follows:

- Advanced industries: 32%
- Business, legal, and professional services: 36%
- Consumer goods and retail: 30%
- Energy and materials: 29%
- Financial services: 42%
- Health care, pharma, and medical products: 33%
- Technology, media, and telecom: 50%[9]

The study further revealed that one-third of respondents were using generative AI in their company in at least one functional area, most commonly marketing and sales, product and service development, and service operations such as customer care and back-office support.

Respondents reported their organization regularly used GenAI in the following given functions:

- Marketing and sales: 14%
- Product and/or service development: 13%
- Service operations: 10%
- Risk: 4%
- Strategy and corporate finance: 4%
- Human resources: 3%
- Supply chain management: 3%
- Manufacturing 2%[10]

Some evidence suggests that GenAI is getting democratized—is becoming more ubiquitous across organizations than previous generations of technology.

In a subsequent study, the McKinsey's Talent Trends Survey conducted across the United States, Canada, and the United Kingdom in July and August 2023, 88% of nontechnical employees (e.g., cashiers, nurses, salespeople, supervisors) said they were using GenAI at work; on the other hand, 12% of technical workers (e.g., developers, programmers, engineers) used generated content in their job.[11]

Following are examples of how different companies have successfully built the foundations of a next generation, AI-empowered company.

GUCCI: CHANGING THE PARADIGM OF CLIENT SERVICES WITH GUCCI 9

First, let's revisit an example we presented earlier: the Italian luxury brand Gucci. Gucci has worked in close partnership with Salesforce for more than 6 years, focused on the goal of "offering customers around the world a direct link with our community, creating a continuous, always authentic experience." The human approach, the investment in the latest technologies, and the aesthetic look and feel of the physical store make Gucci 9 one of the most innovative, inviting, and stylish customer service concepts ever. The core of Gucci's global client service center is using the Salesforce Einstein 1 Platform to generate AI-powered conversational replies for its client advisors.

In the flow of work, from within the Salesforce Service console, advisors are provided with timely AI-assisted service replies that express a "Guccified" brand tone for each customer. The generated replies provide a user-friendly and flexible, yet consistent, conversation framework that advisors can use to enrich their unique interactions with customers. This has helped amplify brand storytelling, moving advisors away from traditional customer service response templates. Additionally, new team members can get versed more quickly in Gucci's unique brand voice, history, and products.

The auto-generated replies also keep client advisors informed and well-versed on Gucci's newest collections. Whether customers engage via a phone conversation, WhatsApp, email, or any digital channel, Gucci makes every interaction personalized with connected customer data.

During the proof of concept phase of the project, which saw a strong collaboration between Gucci 9 and Salesforce Science teams, AI was employed in more than 4,000 AI-powered conversations. Only a few of these interactions required correction, while there was an improvement in commercial performance evidenced by an increase in conversion rates.

> "Our mantra is the human touch powered by technology. Gucci is over 100 years old so there is nothing more sacred than our customers and their data. It is very dear to us. AI is augmenting the life of our advisors and we plan to continue pioneering this in a responsible, ethical and transparent manner with Salesforce."
> —*Vasili Dimitropoulos, Vice President Global Gucci 9 and Product Care Gucci underscores*

Gucci is now exploring AI to deliver targeted recommendations to customers using their own images instead of models, as well as other areas of personalized on-brand support.

L'ORÉAL: LEARNING AND PRIORITIZING INNOVATION USING AI

Cosmetics leader L'Oreal is regarded as an early adopter of AI. The company developed an AI-driven program called TrendSpotter that scans comments, images, and videos across social media to spot emerging fashion trends. By identifying shoppers' interests early, L'Oreal can design and bring products to market faster than competitors, capturing an early mover advantage.[12]

Today L'Oreal's focus is on generative AI to augment marketing across content/creativity, services, search, and consumer care. The company's chief marketing officer recently identified its maturity in this area as being in a "controlled experimentation" phase. The company has developed ethical guidelines for using AI, and it already uses GenAI extensively to create product marketing campaigns. It employs a diverse team of people to oversee model creation and tests to avoid bias and toxicity.[13] At the same time, L'Oreal decided to never use GenAI to build pictures of humans, in order to maintain its integrity as a cosmetics vendor.

The company also launched the L'Oreal Paris Beauty Genius, a GenAI-powered personal beauty advisor app. It provides diagnostic advice, product recommendations, and Q&A on topics that may be uncomfortable to discuss with a live person.[14]

TURTLE BAY RESORT–CUSTOMER 360 DATA FUELING AI TO REINVIGORATE TOURISM

Turtle Bay Resort is the luxury vacation destination nestled on 1,300 acres along Oʻahu's North Shore. The resort saw decreased travel in 2020 and has been looking for ways to reignite revenue ever since. Turtle Bay Resort is on a journey to reinvent itself, heighten awareness of its unique offerings, and establish new, life-long customer relationships. Turtle Bay wants to connect with its customers in a whole new way, empowering its teams to give more personalized attention to guests.

To do so, the resort is leveraging Salesforce's Einstein 1 Platform to build trusted AI capabilities in the flow of work. These insights are fueled by Salesforce Sales Cloud, Service Cloud, Marketing Cloud, and Data Cloud in one platform that will scale and grow with their digital transformation needs over time. Turtle Bay is working to create a comprehensive "Guest 360" of customer profiles for optimal experiences from pre-booking to post-stay, which creates more personalized, holistic customer experiences.

"Our work with Salesforce marks a new chapter for Turtle Bay Resort," said Robert Marusi, chief commercial officer, Turtle Bay Resort. "By leveraging Salesforce's powerful suite of tools through Einstein 1 Platform, we are able to reach new guests with a highly tailored approach to our engagement, ensuring that every guest receives a truly unforgettable experience unique to them."

Turtle Bay Resort is delivering more tailored messages to guests across web, email, and social with Marketing Cloud and has seen a 40% uplift with triple-digit conversion growth through advanced segmentation, personalization, and journey optimization.

Turtle Bay plans to use the Einstein 1 Platform to improve guest experiences even more. An AI assistant will segment customers into ideal personas for hyper-personalized experience recommendations, creating guests for life. Service Replies based on customers' previous interactions will improve front-of-house support efficiency and message consistency. The assistant will also be used to escalate guest cases based on their responses.

NOW IS THE TIME TO PUT AI INTO ACTION

Gucci, L'Oreal, and Turtle Bay Resort are examples of companies using AI successfully today. They are clear about their priorities and have established best practices to experiment with GenAI in a protective yet productive manner that remains true to their company mission.

In line with Isaac Asimov's thesis at the top of this chapter, Harvard Business School Professor Karim Lakhani states that "most companies will not have a choice but to adopt AI . . . at their core functions."[15]

No matter your company's size, industry, or location, it's important to start planning for and participating in GenAI. Yes, there are numerous risks and ethical considerations to consider. That said, the upside impacts are fundamental to a company's ability to compete. Defining safe spaces for using AI and aligning them with human resources is a key component of competitive advantage.

***

Having Faith in the System: How Can We Trust the AI?

Prior generations of AI and ML technology focused on solving discrete tasks, whereas GenAI offers a wide range of diverse use cases and outputs. The downside of this versatility is a higher rate of error and risk. This chapter will explore how we measure and manage these machine-made outputs.

But first, Figure 13.1 shows a personal example from one of your authors (Andrea).

Andrea: *It took me about seven or eight tries and about 20 minutes to craft the prompt to generate the image using OpenAI. It bothers me that the "1 - 2 - 3" is not on one line, but when I tried to make this small tweak it generated an entirely new image with other things I didn't like as much. The stakes of this image not having the text bubble written out exactly as I'd like it here are obviously not that high. But when it comes to running your business and messaging your customers, precision and professionalism are a big deal. After all, the output represents you, and customers will judge you by it.*

HOW EXTENSIVE ARE THE RISKS?

Jobs and Employment. The impact GenAI will have on the workforce concerns many observers. Some structural unemployment is inevitable—meaning, some jobs will be eliminated or changed—so the question becomes whether people can find new, meaningful jobs quickly enough.

FIGURE 13.1   Generating Creative Content with AI
Andrea Lin generated this with DALL-E

The World Economic Forum's most recent *Future of Jobs Report* forecasts that in 5 years people in physically oriented jobs—e.g., equipment operators, truck and bus drivers, and vocational educators—will see the most job growth. On the other hand, administrative jobs such as a data entry clerk, administrative assistants, clerical workers, and bookkeepers would make up the majority of the anticipated job demand declines.[1]

The impact of AI on jobs in 3 to 4 years is likely to be substantial, and people are giving thought to what this might mean for their profession. In February 2024, OpenAI showcased a preview of a tool named Sora's portfolio of 1-minute, high-definition videos generated from natural language prompts, including the following:

- "A person walking down the street in Tokyo"
- "A fly-over of a historic California gold rush town"
- "A happy otter wearing a yellow life jacket surfboarding"[2]

Shortly after that announcement, entertainment mogul Tyler Perry halted investment on an $800 million studio expansion. After seeing samples of Sora's outputs, he was questioning whether film crews, production crews, sound stages, and filming on location will be needed to produce motion picture films in the future.[3]

Bias and Toxicity. AI-generated content has the potential to be damaging. Algorithms were written by engineers, and models are driven by data created by humans. We know the data on the internet are not perfectly free from bias so we must expect the results to reflect this reality. For example, a study from Pennsylvania State University showed that AI models train on data that under-represents populations with disabilities thereby exacerbating social inequalities.[4] How much and how well we filter out bias and toxicity will be a substantial practice area that needs to be developed further.

Bad Actors. In the wrong hands, generated content can be used to create deep fakes, disinformation, and malicious "fake news." Even more concerning is the potential for a cyberattack that succeeds in manipulating a model for its own purpose.

Explainability and Reliability. In many cases, it is very difficult (even impossible) to explain how an answer generated using GenAI was derived. The same prompt yields a variety of responses. Quality of responses and accuracy is difficult to discern. The acceptable margin for error varies by use case.

Auditability. It is challenging to attribute generated content to source data, particularly when using open-source models. Some vendors have offered indemnification to protect original content creators whose work was used for training models. Several high profile lawsuits are in court over copyright infringement including the *New York Times vs. Microsoft and OpenAI, the Author's Guild* *(including George R. R. Martin, John Grisham, and Jody Picoult) vs. OpenAI, Getty Images vs. Stability AI, and Universal Music vs. Anthropic.*

Energy Intensive. Training LLMs requires a substantial amount of computing power and energy, emitting carbon dioxide. The development of foundational models and their proliferation has already had a significant impact on the environment. Based on current data center investment trend estimates, LLMs emit the equivalent of 5 billion US cross-country flights in 1 year.[5]

THE BIGGEST RISK IS IGNORING AI

While these issues are substantial, inaction carries risk. Businesses need to be getting started with GenAI and encouraging exploration across every function. Though it may seem like we are in a sprint already, businesses need to embark on a transformative journey that will take planning, exploration, careful deliberation, and adjusting course over a long period.

The current year or two will be about experimenting with AI safely and raising everyone's AI literacy so that people and companies can use it to its fullest and most optimal potential. This Fourth Industrial Revolution will affect most people personally, socially, and professionally, so preparing ourselves for this adjustment is critical as it is likely the technology adoption curve will accelerate more steeply in 2 to 3 years.

A team of thought leaders, expert researchers, and product managers at Salesforce recently published "Guidelines for Trusted Generative AI" with five focus areas:

Accuracy. Companies need to train models with their own source data. There should be transparency around verifiable results balancing accuracy, precision, and recall as much as there should be clarity when the generated results contain uncertainty. Companies must ensure data are fine-tuned and grounded on models that are accurate, up-to-date, and complete or else the model will confidently create bad content.

Safety. Conduct bias, explainability, and robustness assessments to mitigate bias, toxicity, and harmful outputs. Protect the privacy of personally identifying information (PII) in the data used for training. GenAI models have a risk of leaking the underlying training data either unintentionally or through prompt injection attacks. You must ensure that you are constantly assessing and monitoring your models for prompt injection and data leakage vulnerabilities.

Honesty. Respect data provenance and use models trained on consented data (e.g., open source or user provided). Provide transparency for content generated by AI through proper watermarking or attribution. In a recent survey, the top factor (57% of respondents) to deepen customer trust in AI was greater visibility into its use.[6]

Empowerment. Keep a human at the helm (more on the choice of the word "helm" in a moment) and in a decision-making role, especially when judgment is required to balance augmenting human workers versus automating fully. It should be inclusive and accessible to all. Regardless of the stage of AI development, we must engage in responsible labor practices.

Sustainability. Focus on using the right-sized models to minimize your carbon and water footprint. Sometimes smaller, better-trained models can outperform larger models.[7]

Kathy Baxter, a visiting AI fellow at the National Institute of Standards and Technology and Principal Architect, Responsible AI & Tech at Salesforce, has been a thought leader in this field for many years. She advises:

> We should all strive to create technology that leaves us better off when we use it. It's not enough to have a set of ethical guidelines or principles for employees to follow. They must be supported by a safety culture that rewards employees for highlighting risks of harm, asking not just "can we do this?" but "should we do this?" and implement meaningful consequences when harms are ignored.

HUMANS, WE STILL NEED YOU!

"AI Won't Replace Humans—But Humans With AI Will Replace Humans Without AI"

—Karim Lakhani, Professor at Harvard Business School[8]

Many discussions around the first phase of GenAI have been focused on how copilots and chatbots will augment workers rather than fully automate or replace human jobs. For early adopters, the results have been promising. Human workers for the most part feel empowered and more productive with their time. Many people refer to this practice as having a "human in the loop" insofar as the AI is not running the show.

HUMAN AT THE HELM (HATH) VERSUS HUMAN IN THE LOOP

A recent US-based study of the use of GenAI in the workplace made an interesting finding: an effective AI culture requires that humans are more than just "in the loop." To cultivate trust and build confidence for employees, people should feel accountable for decision-making when using emergent AI outputs and processes.

The researchers believe the phrase "human at the helm" (HATH) helps companies onboard generative AI in a healthy manner. In fact, they have created a *Human at the Helm: Deep Dive & Action Pack* with Best Practices and Interaction Inspiration cards to help you get started. (You can order yours at *humanatthehelm.splashthat.com*.) It seems logical that having a HATH approach will yield many positive outcomes for humans and businesses during this period of significant change.

In practice, studies have also shown that humans partnering with AI have had a significant impact in health care. In Sweden, half of the 80,000 mammograms that were conducted between April 2021 and July 2022 were given to a team of experienced radiologists to be read and the other half were read by AI augmented by a team of radiologists. The second group detected 20% more cancers without an impact on the false positive rate. In addition, the radiologists paired with AI cut their workload in half. The outcome to physicians was a less intense workload, and the outcome to patients was improved early detection of cancers and earlier treatment. This also reduced unnecessary imaging and exposure to radiation.[9]

TYPES OF LLMs

Open-source LLMs are models whose source code, training data, or architecture details are made publicly available. This means anyone can use, modify, and distribute them under a license that is compatible with the open-source definition. They are useful if you don't have in-house resources or ML talent to build your own LLM, which can be cost prohibitive. A more likely path forward is using pre-trained open-source LLMs that are fine-tuned for a specific company's use. This includes enhancing the open-source LLM with company-specific and owned datasets. Some examples would be Meta's LLaMa2, Mistral, and Falcon.

Proprietary LLMs are owned and controlled by an organization so they are not freely available for public use, modification, or distribution. Using a proprietary LLM has less transparency and may take longer to build. They are likely to cost more initially but can potentially cost less at scale. They offer a more controlled environment and higher performance consistency. These proprietary models generate revenue and can be fine-tuned and trained on narrower custom datasets for specific use cases. The outputs could be more specific and reliable with regards to protecting privacy and managing for compliance. Examples include OpenAI's ChatGPT-4.

LLM technology has been born from years of research in academia with influence from industry. The research has been openly available, and the power of people from colleges and startup ventures has helped facilitate a rapid pace of innovation. Open-source communities such as GitHub and Hugging Face have also been fueling this market's explosiveness. Continued openness would be a benefit to more people and companies, but a lot of value comes from those with access to data and models.

Stanford Professor Andrew Ng called AI the "new electricity" back in 2017.[10] Building on that analogy, creating an electric power grid was the responsibility of the government and utility companies, who worked on behalf of communities, rather than something each community had to build for itself.

Databricks announced its general-purpose LLM DBRX on March 27, 2024, which bodes well for the general AI community. It is particularly adept at coding and showed two times faster performance than LLaMA2 while being 40% the size of another leading model (Grok-1) on parameter counts. Databricks announced "every enterprise should have the ability to control its data and its destiny in the emerging world of GenAI."[11]

WHERE IS THE LLM BEING TRAINED?

For the most part, each LLM is designed to be constantly training. It trains on positive or negative feedback it receives after generating content from a prompt. It even trains on the content submitted in the prompt itself. This is why many companies have a policy to not use confidential company information in a GenAI prompt. In the case of OpenAI's consumer service, there is an opt-out option:

> When you use our services for individuals such as ChatGPT, **we may use your content to train our models**. You can opt out of training through our privacy portal by clicking on "do not train on my content," or to turn off training for your ChatGPT conversations, follow the instructions in our Data Controls FAQ.[12]

Open-source models are trained on vast datasets. One large body of work is corpus data, such as books, magazines, websites, academic papers, and even Wikipedia, which is crowd-sourced by whomever feels like contributing. While diversity of styles and content is great, there will be gaps, particularly as you get into subject areas more deeply. So if there is bias in who was able to publish information over the past 100 years, that bias will carry through into the LLM if left unchecked.

Another major component of training data is web-scraped content that crawlers have retrieved. This brings in the most up-to-date content, but some of it may be from a personal website or from copyrighted materials. OpenAI, Microsoft, and Nvidia are being sued for copyright infringement by creators who feel their content was used to train models without sufficient authorization.[13]

THE GenAI SUPPLY CHAIN

If we thought about GenAI as a product we manufacture with quality control guardrails in place, diverse, high-quality data would be the critical raw material. In this supply chain analogy, we rely on the CDP to produce that material into a higher-quality asset. In the Salesforce ecosystem, the Data Cloud is the glue that brings company data together across the customer experience life cycle. It handles the ingestion of data from apps or other external sources that you connect with directly or bring in from a data warehouse or data lake. Then it prepares and transforms the data, maps it to a unified data model, harmonizes the data, and unifies it into insight-filled customer profiles. (See Figure 13.2.)

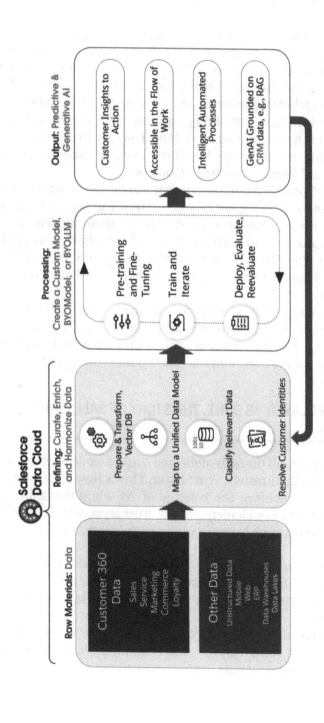

FIGURE 13.2 Salesforce Data Cloud and the Customer Experience Life Cycle

A recent *Fortune* headline read: "Deep learning pioneer Andrew Ng says companies should get 'data-centric' to achieve AI success." In Ng's view, the latest algorithms, LLMs, and code are mostly open and accessible. The real difference is the data a company owns and how those data are gathered, processed, and governed. This becomes a company's most prized, differentiating possession.[14] Most companies don't complain about having not enough data. They suffer from too much fragmented data that are trapped in silos, sometimes hundreds of apps, warehouses, and lakes across the organization.

If you use OpenAI to find recipes that use the ingredients you have on hand in your kitchen, great. If you are trying to use AI to get your business into the fast lane, you need to think about models that use your high octane data in collaboration with or adjacent to publicly available data. You are likely to want to keep options open and keep exploring an assortment of AI models close to your data and close to your business.

For now, companies should be exploring general open-source models enhanced with proprietary data, using RAG for example. It's hard to tell if LLMs will remain as open as they are now in the future, but it would serve the overall market best to maintain openness.

HOW A "TRUST LAYER" IS BUILT: THE STORY OF SALESFORCE (CONTINUED)

The Salesforce AI platform is delivered with a collection of safety guardrails called the Einstein Trust Layer. This is how Salesforce enables customers to achieve the benefits of AI while managing risk. Following are some key elements of the trust layer, which should be incorporated no matter what your ultimate architecture:

- *Prompt masking.* Prompts are protected by masking any PII. In other words, the model doesn't know your specific customer data—it gets masked so the model still has what it needs to get the job done.
- *Zero data retention.* The prompt is sent to your choice of LLM, and if that LLM sits behind an API, the Trust Layer enforces zero data retention, so that your data are never stored outside the platform.

- *Toxicity filter.* On the way back to Salesforce, the Trust Layer employs toxicity detection to ensure the prompt is usable and won't put your brand at risk.
- *Auditing.* The prompt, the response, and the scoring are logged in a secure audit trail, and they power reinforcement learning based on your outcomes for models that Salesforce hosts, or whose weights you own.

Working on your data and AI capability is not a destination. Methods need to be cultivated over time in a systematic way. Your AI needs to be fed accurate, timely data over time that is free from bias. Likewise, filtering toxicity is a key to propagating successful results in your models. Having a human at the helm who has incentives to provide feedback and guidance is another critical success factor.

Do the due diligence to investigate the technologies you are using and know what safeguards they have in place to handle customer information. Understand how they handle lineage, and be sure there is an audit trail so you can learn from mistakes. Having a Trust Layer in place means you can have more trust in the outcome.

***

CHAPTER 14

Data Collaboration—A Rising Imperative

The term "co-opetition" was coined in the mid-1990s to describe the strategy of collaborating with your competitors. While examples were few at that time, the concept has gained traction, particularly in markets that are sizable and where a substantial growth opportunity could benefit both parties.

In 2008, UPS agreed to partner with rival DHL when DHL was struggling to enter the US market successfully. In part, UPS chose to partner because it had extra capacity along its routes that would make the partnership profitable. Likewise, the risk of DHL working with FedEx instead could have been debilitating to both UPS and DHL. Game theorists could draw an impressive graph to calculate the risks and rewards. They could also show that competitors sharing strengths can yield results greater than either would realize on their own. Despite potential risks, more and more businesses are using co-opetition as a formula for speed, differentiation, and market leadership.

With the data gold rush accelerating, it is apparent that product and go-to-market partnerships are proliferating among high tech rivals. Microsoft and Apple, Nvidia and Oracle, Snowflake and Nvidia, Microsoft and OpenAI, . . . Google and Apple are in discussions over using Google's AI assistant, Gemini, on the next macOS. In fact, the fear of missing out (FOMO) is high if you are a big tech player not included among a hot handful of partnerships.

Competitors across industries are also vying to stay atop the news headlines. Companies want to be associated with innovation and generative AI to win the mindshare of their customers and prospects.

Collaborations between adjacent vendors are solidifying companies' momentum while boxing-out newcomers or other competitors trying to gain ground.

We previously discussed the importance of unifying one's own fragmented data for strategic advantage. What if companies enriched their data further by cross-pollinating it with strategic partners to create a superset of data? The next frontier is finding and sharing data with willing partners and collaborating in a privacy-compliant manner.

GOODBYE TO BROWSER-BASED THIRD-PARTY COOKIES

Digital advertisers used third-party cookies for many years to acquire new audiences. Apple and Mozilla were the first to deprecate third-party cookies from their browsers back in 2017. Google, which has 65% of the worldwide browser market share has—after several delays—begun the process of eliminating third-party cookies from its browsers.

While done primarily for privacy reasons, third-party cookie deprecation will likely benefit larger intermediaries with the greatest scale, namely, Google and Apple, as well as the larger so-called walled gardens such as Meta, owner of Facebook and Instagram. Advertising budgets will likely be focused on direct server-side alternatives owned by these gardens and destinations like Google (i.e., YouTube, Google Search). To many advertisers, cookie loss represents a major shakeup of the $700 billion digital ad business. Many have been scrambling to find new methods to reach new audiences with attribution.

Advertisers are trying to find and adopt reliable methods of reach that yield reasonable economics around return on advertising spending (ROAS) and cost of customer acquisition (CAC). In the consumer space, CAC has risen by more than 60% over the past decade.[1] On a per dollar basis, ad-based links are less effective and with less traceability, so companies are shifting that dollar spend to achieve higher return on investment elsewhere, where possible.

Advertisers are addressing the cookieless environment in three ways:

1. Companies are trying to get better at collecting first-party data as a key strategic business practice.
2. Marketers in particular are pursuing data-sharing partnerships and more collaboration through emerging solutions.

3. Companies are implementing and using data platform technologies such as CDPs to harmonize and orchestrate activations across the Customer 360.

COLLECT FIRST-PARTY DATA AS A STRATEGIC DIFFERENTIATOR

Consent management platforms (CMPs) allow web and mobile app publishers to collect first-party data in a privacy-aware manner. Consumers experience CMP pop-up windows providing the choice to opt in to essential cookies (required to use a service such as an email) or to all cookies (including optional uses such as analytics and tracking).

These enterprise-grade platforms also have consent management tools to accommodate different market requirements, which could include geographic or industry-oriented parameters to maintain compliance. Many CMPs such as OneTrust or Didomi can integrate with the Google Tag Manager and other tags to comply with users' opt-in or opt-out preferences.

Another method of building first-party data comes from investing in server-side data collection. With browser or client-side event tracking diminishing, advertisers are turning to server-side tracking and conversion APIs in response. Because all of this data is collected on advertisers' internal servers, marketers have the flexibility and reliability of the data from internal servers running the apps and websites themselves. CMPs also support compliance with key global regimes such as General Data Protection Regulation (GDPR) and Data Subject Access Request (DSAR) in the EU, and California Consumer Privacy Act (CCPA). We will explore the role of various regulations further in the next chapter.

Implementing conversion APIs takes technical expertise, such as API linking, and time to set up and maintain on each platform. However, conversion APIs are not compatible with every media platform yet. For those with the bandwidth, a company can use Google Tag Manager (GTM) for server-side tagging that stores data in a Google Cloud container. With conversion APIs, key events on- and offline collected server-side are considered first party data. This can be shared (for example) with Meta by setting up an endpoint such as Facebook's Conversion API.[2]

Companies using conversion APIs can select what level of data to share. This feature allows for granularity that can be more cost effective. They can also opt to transform the data before passing it along to vendors. This may mean anonymizing or masking certain data types to protect customers' privacy. While it can be somewhat burdensome to manage a web of connectors, companies have benefited from behavioral data insights that lead to improved ROAS.

As we suggested in Chapter 5, asking for consent and earning genuine trust from consumers are different things. In a recent Pew Research Center survey conducted across US audiences, 78% of US adults said they "trust themselves to make the right decisions about their personal information." However, 61% are "skeptical that anything they do will make much difference." Furthermore, only 21% were "confident that those who have access to their personal information will do what is right."[3]

Building a brand that consumers trust with their data is a business model and cultural hurdle to overcome. Headlines such as Amazon's and Meta's fines for violating European Union regulations in 2021 and 2023 foster an atmosphere of doubt. Notably, figuring out how to earn a customer's trust is a competitive differentiator.

PURSUE DATA SHARING AND COLLABORATION

Another area of focus for advertisers seeking first-party data has been spending more on performance marketing outcomes instead of impressions. Retail media networks (RMNs) have been the beneficiary. Amazon is the leader in this market with almost $50 billion in ad revenue. Market spending on RMNs doubled in recent years and is growing quickly.[4]

Retailers such as Walmart, Target, Home Depot, and Best Buy are also trying to take advantage of RMNs with sponsored ad space on their own websites. Consumer packaged-goods companies are advertising more on RMNs to feature products closer to the web point of sale. They can also take advantage of physical and web-based behavioral first-party data. While generally positive on RMNs, experts caution that sponsored space should be kept in check and carefully balanced against the retailer's brand and user experience.

Adjacent services markets such as data clean rooms (DCRs) are gaining momentum while facilitating value from RMN investments. DCRs are environments where different companies can share and collaborate using first-party data without providing access to that data in its raw form. Private data are anonymized, aggregated, and matched in the DCR.

For example, Amazon Marketing Cloud (AMC) offers a cloud-based clean room that integrates with Amazon's demand-side platform (DSP) for campaign analytics and measurement. Advertisers' RMN data "meets" Amazon's data in a clean room. The offspring of the two companies' data is an integrated, sanitized dataset that provides advertisers with an aggregated view of post-campaign analytics or audience activation while also being privacy compliant.

Most recently Amazon announced it was expanding its clean room service to include in-store attribution using Whole Foods data.[5] Advertisers benefit by having more clarity around how their spending on Amazon media contributes to direct to customer conversions. And so RMNs combined with DCRs are a growing area of data collaboration and exploration. Google Ads Data Hub (ADH) is another clean room service that is inherently tied to Google Cloud Platform, including Google BigQuery.

Along the same lines, major retailers such as Walmart have partnered with independent ad-tech firm The Trade Desk to develop a demand-side platform—e.g., Walmart DSP. This gives Walmart access to The Trade Desk's inventory across numerous categories and draws on shopper data from Walmart's channels of engagement, both online and brick and mortar.

Disney, with a vast canvas of media inventory across many services such as Disney+, launched its own clean room capabilities a few years ago. One of Disney's partners was Snowflake (which acquired the startup DCR Samooha in 2023). Disney has since added clean room interoperability with AWS and Google Cloud to form a marketplace for first-party data insights.

In addition, Disney Portal was launched in combination with the DCR Habu to support general marketers.[6] Disney claims its DCR has a high match rate and that it provides the ability to create "lookalike" audiences, similar to those in the advertisers' own first-party dataset. A key success factor for clean rooms is the combination of activation and measurement in one workstream so that brands can make incremental adjustments to target more accurately and generate better ROAS.

Habu, a provider of self-service DCRs, was acquired by LiveRamp in 2024. Habu specializes in data collaboration with Google Ads Data Hub,

Amazon Marketing Cloud, and Meta. Habu's focus on data collaboration combined with LiveRamp's activation connections (in ad tech and media partners) and RampID identity solution helps apply enriched collaborative data to both insights and actions. (See Figure 14.1.)

On the RMN side, grocery retailers have been particularly active. For example, Albertson's joined a Pinterest collaboration platform and created their own RMN called the Albertson's Media Collective. The collaboration led to a clean dataset that allowed Albertson's advertising customers to reach their audiences on Pinterest prior to entering the grocery store. Once these consumers are in store, Albertsons would prompt visitors to use in-store promotions to acquire data via Albertson's app. Albertson's media customers, who are generally packaged goods company advertisers, hope to use multi-touch attribution to increase ad spend efficacy.[7] In this scenario, Pinterest and Albertson's are both publishers and a consumer packaged-goods company would be a third company added into the data clean room partnership.

Today in most clean room scenarios, one side of the collaboration is almost always a RMN or media company like Disney or NBCU. But a DCR could represent any two or more companies seeking to collaborate in a privacy-safe manner. Use cases range from enriching customer profiles, analyzing and expanding audiences, to scoring segments' predictive behaviors. For example, a high-end SUV manufacturer might collaborate with an outdoor luxury clothing retailer in a

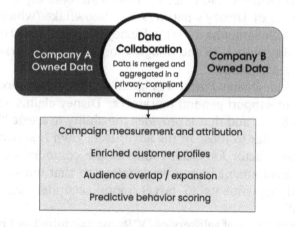

FIGURE 14.1 Schematic of a Data Clean Room

DCR to find similar customers, and a new audience could be created for an SUV campaign with a fashion theme. That audience could then be found on a large platform like Meta using the SUV manufacturer's own prospect database.

As we've seen, DCRs are different from traditional partnerships where companies exchange user data outright. With data clean rooms, user-level data never leaves the environment; only aggregated insights and reports are returned. And while these data collaborations have a lot of power, the complexity and scope of administering them is not accessible to every company today.

CIRCLING BACK TO THE CDP

As we pointed out previously, in addition to actively managing consent and data collaboration, Customer 360 professionals are leaning into the CDP. Although we've discussed this topic before (and also wrote a book about it we may have mentioned once or twice), in the context of DCRs the question often arises: If you have a clean room do you still need a CDP? And if you have a CDP, do you already have a clean room?

CDPs and clean rooms are similar in the sense that they both handle customer data and they both improve personalization—or what we'd call the Customer 360. The main difference is that the data in the CDP belong to you—the user—whereas in a DCR, only some of it does. The purpose of a CDP is to provide access to first-party data at the customer level. On the other hand, DCRs exist to *prevent* access to first-party data at the customer level. These technologies are complementary: the CDP is the logical source of first-party data to provide to the DCR.

With the zero-copy and zero-ETL capabilities of some CDPs—and solutions like Salesforce Data Cloud expanding its Zero Copy Partner Network—the possibility of two or more customers collaborating to create and share a derived or "clean" dataset in a privacy compliant manner to enrich audiences is within reach.

DATA AS A CORE DISCIPLINE

According to a recent MuleSoft Connectivity Benchmark Report, 28% of the hundreds of applications in the average enterprise have some degree of connectivity to another internal system. It's no wonder that 81% of IT leaders report that data silos are hindering their digital transformation efforts.[8]

The imperative of a CDP is to collect trapped data, unify it, and use it in a strategic manner. A data platform should be able to receive data from common systems—like email, website (tag management, content management systems), mobile apps, e-commerce, analytics (Adobe and Google), point-of-sale (stores, event venues), and enterprise data warehouses and data lakes.

All of these data should be zero- or first-party information your company owns, or (in some cases) it could be shared or acquired. In any case, the data should be applied using closely tracked consumer consent parameters. Consent is legally enforced in many places and contexts, and even when it isn't, customers expect consideration.

As technologies improve, enterprises are in a better position to be open to data sharing and collaboration. Moreover, technologies like DCRs (coupled with CDPs and CMPs) are able to provide a trusted environment for collaboration. Synthetic datasets are also increasingly useful. Enriching data with partners will become more important where third-party data becomes less available and usable.

Companies must simultaneously sharpen the utility of their data as a differentiator for connecting with customers while meeting the rising bar of having full respect for customer privacy. Collaboration is a new lever for competitive advantage, and co-opetition is back.

***

CHAPTER 15

Privacy, Compliance, and Consent

Tension between privacy and personalization is apparent. It's not logically possible to provide a personalized experience to customers—no matter how talented your Customer 360 team and how sophisticated its technology—if you don't know anything about them. If you know a little, you can personalize a little, and so on. The end state is an experience like being a long-time customer of Amazon or Netflix, where every recommendation is almost uncanny. Why? It's built on more data.

But are customers aware of this tension? Not exactly. As we've seen a number of times already, customers tend to want or expect relevance (which implies some level of knowledge) but are often reluctant to share data. As an example, a recent BCG survey showed that 62% of consumers say they want marketing that's personalized to their interests; meanwhile, fully 45% say they are "uncomfortable" sharing personal data to receive personalized experiences.[1]

A trusted relationship with customers is a company's gateway to securing critical first-party data. The importance of this relationship is only increasing; consumers are more cautious and even skeptical when asked to share information or opt in to data collection. Increased respect for consumer privacy is forcing companies to adapt and innovate. Today, Customer 360 practitioners know they must *earn* the right to their customers' data.

In this chapter, we'll browse the state of consumer privacy and the regulatory environment. Key success factors such as consent and compliance strategies will be a key priority, as will platform technology enablers.

Digital data privacy is maintained by four parties with (at times) different agendas:

1. Web browsers and standards bodies—that want to protect themselves from legal exposure and provide a product (the browser) that meets the needs of its users (consumers)
2. Government regulators—who presumably act on behalf of legal principles to serve the people they govern
3. Consumers—who want to protect their data, while providing enough to get the experiences and services they want
4. Companies—that want to maintain productive and delightful relationships with customers, while obeying all relevant regulations

Let's take a brief look at recent trends within the first two groups.

WEB BROWSERS AND STANDARDS BODIES

Browsers and operating systems (which run apps on mobile devices and TVs) are your customers' gateways to the connected digital world. So what the owners of these browsers and operating systems decide to do will always have a big impact on your Customer 360.

Browsers adhere to protocols that are developed through a process managed by the World Wide Web Consortium (known as the W3C), which has overseen internet standards such as HTML from the beginning. Browsers also adopt their own standards and methods, both as competitive differentiation and to meet the needs of their users, as they perceive them. Both browsers and standards bodies are therefore outsize players in the digital customer data conversation.

The browser market is highly concentrated, with Google's Chrome browser commanding more than 65% global share and Apple's Safari a distant number two, with a roughly 18% share. Microsoft's Edge, which uses Google's open-source Chromium technology, and Mozilla's Firefox each command 5% and 3% shares, respectively.

Apple's Safari has always maintained a more privacy-focused posture with respect to data collection, particularly by advertisers, publishers, and advertising technology vendors. Since its inception, the Safari browser has blocked third-party tracking cookies by default.

Intelligent tracking prevention: Safari privacy protections took a more stringent turn in 2017 with the launch of Intelligent Tracking Prevention (ITP), which sought to suppress various techniques ad tech companies used to identify users. Later versions of the protocol clamped down on techniques such as redirects and link decoration used to fill gaps left by third-party cookie deprecation. Then Apple announced a mandatory opt-in for its Identifier for Advertisers (IDFA), used by mobile application publishers, signaling its reluctance to allow much user-level tracking in future.

Enhanced tracking prevention and Brave: Mozilla announced a similar policy to Apple's with the launch of its Enhanced Tracking Prevention (ETP). While Mozilla's stance is not as stringent by default as Apple's, the Brave browser takes a privacy-first position as a competitive differentiator, generally blocking ads by default and allowing ads directly enabled by the user.

Google's Chrome and AdID: In 2020, Google announced that the third-party cookie would expire in 2022. After two delays, Google officially began restricting third-party cookies for subsets of Chrome users starting in 2024. Similarly, Google announced the phase-out of its mobile app identifier, called AdID.

The Privacy Sandbox: For a number of years, Google and others have contributed privacy-safe post-cookie solution ideas to the Privacy Sandbox. This is Google's test bed for a set of open standards designed to enhance privacy on the web while still offering marketers ad targeting and measurement within the Chrome browser.

A large number of ideas have passed through the Privacy Sandbox, and most have not survived scrutiny—as expected. On the targeting side, solutions tend to aggregate large numbers of browsers and tag them with useful labels (hypothetically: "cat lover" or "fashionista") while taking elaborate statistical precautions not to expose any individual. On the measurement side, aggregate and anonymized results are reported. Personal information tends to stay in the users' own browser, and techniques such as randomization and added noise preserve privacy.

Even without browser-based cookies, any kind of data collection will likely require consent in the future. In order to comply with laws such as the General Data Protection Regulation (GDPR) in the European Union, for example, companies must meet a series of conditions to store and track user data. Such disclosures include purpose, intended use, duration of storage, ability to revoke consent, and auditability. In 2023, Google Consent Mode introduced a signal collection tool that offers advertisers aggregated data from Google tags. It uses full or anonymized data depending on users' consent selection.

GOVERNMENT REGULATORS

Legislatures around the world remain eager to enact regulations related to digital data collection and use. The European Union's ePrivacy-related GDPR has resulted in some high-profile fines and widespread opt-in requirements for internet browsers. Other regions followed suit, e.g., the Australian Competition and Consumer Commission, which recently firmed up that country's protections, and the Brazilian General Data Privacy Law (LGPD). In the US, the California Consumer Protection Act (CCPA) was rolled out in mid-2020 and many other states followed suit.

The so-called "Seven Principles" of GDPR were described in Article 5 of the legislation:

- Transparency: The consumer should know what data are being collected, by whom.
- Purpose limitation: Data can only be used for the explicit purpose granted by the consumer.
- Data minimization: Only as much (and no more) data can be collected to serve the purpose noted previously.
- Accuracy: Self-explanatory.
- Storage limitation: Data can be retained for only a limited time.
- Security: Data must be stored in a way that they can't be accessed by unauthorized parties.
- Accountability: The data "controller" (legally defined) must provide ability to audit and edit data

The European Commission introduced laws related to cross-border data flows in 2023, so companies must now pay closer attention to cross-border data sharing. And the Data Privacy Framework was enacted to ensure data shared between the United States and the European Union is done safely and legitimately.[2] This replaces the previous Privacy Shield, which allowed European citizen data to be stored by US companies in US data centers. The United States only has rights to EU data that are "necessary and proportionate," putting more scrutiny on personal data that cross continents.

GenAI has also stressed the foundations of GDPR. The EU Artificial Intelligence Act was passed to protect individual rights and privacy, and it also sets boundaries to counter risks in areas such as finance, justice, and employment. Key tenets are data transparency (what data are used and why) and accountability (who owns and controls the data).

While reasonable enough, these principles in practice place a tremendous burden on the Customer 360 professional not only to collect consent alongside data, but also to provide the necessary technical infrastructure to support compliance and auditing. Such infrastructure is already becoming simply a cost of doing business online.

At a practical level, we approach privacy and compliance as a three-tiered practice:

1. Classify data—assigning data ownership, field usage, field status, and metadata such as data sensitivity level
2. Determine user entitlements—role-based entitlements and governance to data, internal and external (i.e., customer-facing)
3. Ensure compliance—auditing and persistence; ability to analyze compliance

Ultimately, privacy is about building a trusted relationship with customers. As we have seen, customers have shown that they *will* share data with *trusted partners*. The key phrase here is "trusted partners." In a 2023 Salesforce report, 80% of customers said they would more likely trust a company with personal data if its use were clearly explained.[3]

Building trust has elements that can be incorporated into a MarTech architecture. Its components are the following:

- Consent: "Get my permission."
- Restriction of processing: "Stop processing my data."
- Right to be forgotten: "Delete my data."
- Data subject requests: "What information do you have about me?"
- Security: "Prevent unauthorized access to my data."
- Data use preferences: "This is what I am okay with."

BUILDING TRUST

To build—or rebuild—trust with consumers is critical to collecting and using their data for personalization. Consumers will share data with brands they trust. In fact, the data advantage of certain brands is their competitive edge, the very thing that keeps their customers coming back. People regularly share their most intimate data with Facebook (family photos), Amazon (purchases), LinkedIn (job searches), Google (search history), Stitch Fix (waist sizes)—and many more—because the personalization and responsive experience they receive makes it worthwhile. They trust these brands.

But as our grandmothers said (or should have said), trust is something that is earned and not bought. Building trust is a multi-pronged effort:

- *Reliability*—data security and uptime; patching and maintenance
- *Legality*—legal compliance and the flexibility to adapt to regulatory changes
- *Transparency*—transparent collection and use of customer data
- *Value*—sufficient benefits received for exchange

An additional requirement is more existential: corporate ethics. Part of customers' comfort with data sharing resides in their feelings about a company's general trustworthiness, which includes perceptions about their behaviors in the world and corporate ethics. For their part, many corporations are taking steps to improve their privacy perception or "brand" with customers.

So it's clear we're at a pivotal moment: consumers are inherently mistrustful, governments are taking action, and companies are on the hook to deliver personalization while maintaining a trusted, transparent relationship. It's the new reality for customer data.

FOUR PRIVACY TACTICS TO TRY

Customer 360 teams are going to have to master the art of gaining consumer trust. How? Following are some general guidelines from the research:

1. Don't talk about people behind their backs

It turns out that we don't like this behavior online any more than we do at work or school. Our attitudes toward information sharing depend both on the type of information and the way it's shared, what social scientists call the "information flows." One study found we are much more comfortable with open, direct so-called "first-person sharing" than we are with covert "third-party sharing." The latter, when disclosed, actually drove down purchase interest by 24%. Conversely, using "overt data collection" *can restore interest* and rebuild trust.

Bottom line: tell people directly how you are gathering their data.

2. Give a sense of control

Like Janet Jackson, we really want "control." An alarming 81% of respondents to a Pew Research survey confessed they felt they had almost "no control" over companies collecting their data.[4] This feeling is rife in the United States. When consumers in the United States and European Union were asked if they would opt out of data collection in the future, US consumers were 1.5 times more likely to say "yes."[5] Why? One likely explanation is that, for all its fits and starts, GDPR provides a sense of control. In America, our hodgepodge of legislation and tools does not. People have been shown to share data much more willingly when they believe they can control what they share, even if that control is an illusion.

Bottom line: help customers believe they control the data.

3. Explain the benefits in concrete, positive terms

It's up to the enterprise to describe the privacy value exchange as concretely and positively as they can. The insight here is that concrete benefits might often dominate abstract risks—and that privacy "threats" are usually abstract. But stay positive and benefit focused because evidence suggests that mentioning risks makes people nervous. The idea is to give the consumer a sense of the awesomeness of your personalized experience, either in words or pictures. In one study, for example, an ad for a rental company using a person's physical location performed better when it was explained that location data were used specifically to mention services not available elsewhere.

Bottom line: paint a happy picture of tangible benefits for sharing data.

4. Remember, people are different

It is often assumed that attitudes to online privacy and ad targeting are demographically determined. Millennials and Gen Z are the cultural paranoids, while boomers and GenX are more relaxed. It turns out these attitudes are more a function of our personalities than our demos: they're a state of mind. Some years ago, the Advertising Research Foundation released a report on "ad receptivity" that concluded that the anti-ad crowd were more likely to be "suspicious" and "headstrong." And a different study identified about one-third of the online population as "privacy actives," more informed and aware. Rather than retreating from data sharing, these "actives" were two times more likely to share their purchase history in exchange for better recommendations.

So, the privacy conversation will be different with different groups, and these groups are likely not segmented by age, gender, or income. The "actives" just need more information and the more, the better. The "rejecters" need their suspicions allayed. It's up to the Customer 360 team to figure out which psychographic segment each consumer inhabits.

Bottom line: throw your customer insights and data science teams at the problem.

And remember, you can always try something new. Ask people to share data after you've given them something of value. Be explicit. Ask them how they feel. Give them the remote.

The human rules still apply: trust is something that is earned, not just given.

***

CHAPTER 16

Next-generation Analytics for the Enterprise

"Hey Siri, do I have enough money left in my grocery budget to buy everything on my list?"

If you purchase everything on your list, based on average prices of historical visits, you would exceed your grocery budget by $37.

"Whoa, what happened to all my money?"

I see three transactions around the 22nd of August that are outliers deviating from your normal behavior. One transaction for a bakery, one for a brewery, and one for the grocery store. They are each either atypical expenses or atypical amounts.

"What was going on around that time?"

You had nine events on your calendar around that time. However, the most obvious explanation for these costs would be an event titled "Mitchell's birthday party." That would coincide with a requirement for baked goods, adult beverages, and additional groceries.

"Can you send payment requests to the attendees, except Mitchell, for their share of the expenses?"

I have sent Venmo payment requests for one-fourth of the cost, or $48.32, to Kyra, Will, Sumana, and Adam.

"Can you watch for situations like this in the future and check with me if I need to be paid back before I run out of money?"

I will monitor your transactions for outliers related to an event and prompt you for permission to send payment requests for reimbursement.

It's easy to imagine next generation analytics for the enterprise by reimagining consumer experiences that we live every day. For example, this person is just managing his life; he is not *trying* to do analytics. He isn't thinking about the relationship between his budgeting app, grocery list, bank data, grocery prices, calendar data, or payment data. He isn't jumping between disparate applications or sending requests to IT to modify a dashboard. He is just using natural language to interact with AI to plan, ask, understand, act, and monitor.

You might be thinking, "Wait, that isn't how we are using analytics today," and you wouldn't be alone. The previous example should largely be considered "future state," but we are on the precipice of an analytics evolution. The analytics market is embarking on a transformative period that will change the way that people interact with data, lower the barrier of entry to user engagement, and ultimately will democratize data-driven decision-making.

In this chapter, we will discuss the current analytics landscape, the rise of "consumer-based" analytics, and how technologies are evolving toward proactive analytics in the flow of work.

THE STATE OF TODAY'S ANALYTICS LANDSCAPE

In 2006, British mathematician Clive Humby presciently coined the phrase, "Data is the new oil."[1] This widely referenced phrase aptly reflects the increasing volume and velocity of data we've seen produced in the last 20 years. In Chapter 8, we referenced this prolific acceleration of data generation, the impact it has on organizations and how it has fueled the pace of innovation.

This data explosion has directly impacted the analytics market as organizations seek to harness and make productive use of the information they are collecting. According to Gartner, the current analytics platform market is a $32B industry and forecasted to double to more than $60B by 2027.[2] This classification includes everything from business intelligence (BI) and analytics platforms, to enterprise reporting tools, data science technologies, location intelligence suites, and domain-specific analytics offerings.

Yet, despite the general acknowledgement that data are core differentiators, along with the corresponding increase in spend on analytics investments, we continue to observe that the vast majority of organizations are struggling to become data-driven. A recent IDC survey is evidence of this phenomenon and highlights these gaps (see Figure 16.1).

The conclusion of this study was wide ranging in terms of the *why*, but among the core contributors included the following:

- **Lack of reach:** Even with the rise of modern low/no code analytics tools, the ability to conduct analysis remains largely confined to a handful of "skilled" users. This limits the ability to provide domain-relevant insights to the majority of business users.
- **Lack of skills:** Using modern analytics platforms requires significant training and proprietary solution expertise. This creates a high barrier of entry and requires significant time and expertise to upskill.
- **Lack of Trust:** Too many disparate applications and toolsets facilitate data silos. Knowledge workers often don't know where to go to answer their question, if the data are up to date, or if they are accurate.
- **Lack of Scale:** The sheer volume of data is overwhelming. Most users are limited to accessing data within a particular application, limited by data size, or restricted by the types of questions that can be asked.

What Executives Want	What Executives Have
83% of CEOS want their organizations to be more data driven	**33%** are comfortable questioning KPIs and metrics used in organinzations
87% of CXOs said being an intelligent enterprise is their top priority	**29%** are asked to communicate using data-driven methods
	30% say actions are driven by data analysis
	34% find it easy to find internal or external collaborators that can help

FIGURE 16.1 State of Data-Driven Organizations
Source: Ashutosh Gaur, "Tableau WhitePaper US47605621 FINAL-2," Scribd, n.d., https://www.scribd.com/document/520024650/Tableau-WhitePaper-US47605621-FINAL-2

These are just a few of the reasons that indicate we still have a long way to go to uplift the analytical proficiency across the typical organization. The good news is that emerging technological enhancements are rapidly fueling new enhancements to expand analytics adoption. This will deliver entirely new solutions to help engage more users across the enterprise, enhance data governance, enforce trust in data, and will fundamentally change how organizations think about data and analytics.

So, what are a few of these emerging trends?

THE RISE OF "CONSUMER-BASED" ANALYTICS

Today, Tableau is widely considered the market leader in the business intelligence and analytics market. Fifteen years ago, it redefined the business intelligence industry by pioneering the concept of "self-service" analytics. Its patented VizQL technology provided a low/no code, drag-and-drop user experience that largely shifted the analytics market from what was traditionally an "IT-centric" reporting function, to a more agile, "business user–centric" approach.

Yet even with modern analytics tools, significant barriers to adoption remain. Extracting value from data requires intimate knowledge of the backend data, a requisite level of technical ability, and the domain knowledge required to ask and get answers to the key questions. This limits the vast majority of users in an organization, who end up as *consumers* of data and still rely on data analysts and engineers with the right skills to extract data value and communicate insights.

With the recent enhancements of GenAI, combined with more traditional augmented intelligence techniques, we're beginning to see the emergence of a new class of analytics often referred to as "consumer-based" analytics. These experiences will fundamentally shift how we define self-service analytics and will broaden analytics adoption across the enterprise. Several innovations are fueling this "consumer-based" approach.

Conversational UX. Analytics is no longer just a one way stream of communication, where a user sends individual queries to a source to return an output. With the advent of GenAI and LLMs that are grounded in relevant business data and metadata, the analysis process is becoming a conversational exercise. Users are able to engage with the system in natural language and ask follow-up questions without the loss of context from previous discussions. This opens up entirely new ways to conduct data discovery, without necessarily requiring deep product expertise or intimate knowledge of the data back-end structure. For example, a marketer could ask in plain language, "Which products are my highest sellers?" to which the system would produce a visualization, a metric, or perhaps even ask for clarification. The user could then immediately drill down by asking for a regional, market, or segment breakdown as if the user were having a conversation with a data analyst.

AI as an "assistant." Today, even the most simple data analysis still requires knowledge of the product fundamentals. Historically, making use of analytics tooling has required substantial time and energy to learn the tools via resources like hands-on training courses, how-to articles, and community forums. In the not-too-distant future, every knowledge worker will be able to leverage AI as a "personal assistant" to help not only expedite the learning curve, but to also help identify trends, highlight anomalies, and teach a user *how* to use certain analysis techniques.

For example, Einstein CoPilot for Tableau leverages AI models that have been grounded with best practices and collective user community knowledge to not only do things like generate code syntax and auto-mate the visualization process, but more importantly, to *educate* by guiding users through the data preparation and analysis process and suggest ways to optimize the output.

Insight automation. With improvements in AI-driven automated insights, the system can now help automate repetitive analyst activities and help with the recognition of patterns and trends to improve effi-ciencies and expedite time to value. This will not only help analysts be more productive, but it will help those without deep analytics exper-tise to receive personalized, domain-relevant insights they otherwise wouldn't have been able to identify.

EVOLVING FROM *REACTIVE* TO *PROACTIVE* ANALYTICS

Historically, data initiatives treated data analysis and visualization as the end goal. It was considered the valuable part of the process that was extracted as the last step in the data pipeline. This process has required considerable levels of time and effort to progress from raw data to tangible insights which ultimately are conveyed in some form of a query, report, metric, or visual. Figure 16.2 demonstrates a generic vision of this left-to-right analytics life cycle.

Increasingly, the analytics life cycle is shifting from something that produces insights that are often consumed passively, to becoming a *proactive* process that serves as a mechanism to take action on insight. For example, any particular data value might be used to build a customer churn model, product recommendation engine, customer support chatbot, packaged and sold as a data product, or even as a trigger for personalized marketing emails.

Think back to that first consumer example where the user checked his budget and sent payment requests. Imagine it now in a business context:

> **"Einstein, I just received a travel approval request for my employee to go to a conference. Do I have enough money left in my budget for this?"**
>
> *If you approve this request, based on their submitted estimates, you would exceed your budget by $3,700.*
>
> **"Whoa, what happened to all my money, I thought I had wiggle room?"**
>
> *The team offsite you attended in Q1 had several entertainment and meal expenses allocated to the whole team that exceeded the planned amount.*
>
> **"Can you find room anywhere else? There are some big opportunities on the line at this event, and I think we should be there."**
>
> *You could reallocate the money you had set aside to buy the team sweatshirts, or as the budget rolls up to your manager, you could see if*

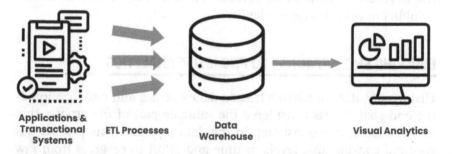

Applications & Transactional Systems   ETL Processes   Data Warehouse   Visual Analytics

FIGURE 16.2 The Conventional Analytics Life Cycle

any of your peers have budget to spare. Or there are five other confer-ences already approved for the year; perhaps you could reduce the num-ber of attendees, or attend virtually.

"From now on, when you see a team meal on the calendar, can you update me with the budget we have available for that event so I can make decisions before I spend the money?"

I will monitor your calendar for team events and notify you in advance of your remaining budget. I can also help give recommen-dations of venues that would fit your budget based on other travel's expense reports.

This example illustrates what we mean by analytics as a proactive exercise. The user in this example is no longer just passively tracking their progress on a dashboard, or consuming a KPI. They are able to communicate proactively to anticipate a problem *before* it occurs. This ends up creating mechanisms to put safeguards in place to mitigate risk all while leading to informed decisions that impact *future* results.

So how close are we to this reality? Closer than you might think. Consider the elements of this proactive experience that already exist today:

- Natural language query (NLQ)—The user is able to exchange con-versationally with the system in natural language to both extract insights and communicate an action. With the advent of LLMs supplemented by techniques like RAG (retrieval augmented gen-eration) to infuse relevant, nuanced data into these models, NLQ can increasingly handle more complex tasks and queries.
- Data federation—The data used in this case may have existed dis-parately across a heterogeneous data environment. With the advent of the modern data fabric combined with cloud platforms' ability to process and store greater volumes of data than ever before, inte-grating and establishing a relationship between data entities has never been easier.
- Data observability—The user was able to use an analytics endpoint as a way to trigger events. In this case, a workflow was created to proactively monitor, track, and alert the user when data reached a particular threshold. With modern AI techniques, the ability to identify issues and accelerate error resolution will become easier than ever.

- Real-time analytics—Modern data platforms make real-time decisioning possible. Data are queried "live" against the backend database to ensure users can access the most up-to-date intelligence regardless of data type and data volume minimizing the need for stale data extracts or data duplication to handle scale.

ANALYTICS IN THE FLOW OF WORK

As a data consumer, the most difficult part of analysis is often just finding the relevant data, knowing where to look to locate the most up to date analysis, or figuring out how to best share insights with colleagues. These pain points often lead to a lack of user engagement, facilitate spreadsheet silos, and the inability to service a large swath of the organization with data.

Today, organizations are increasingly expecting *more* from a consumer standpoint. The modern worker is expecting analysis to be a personalized, collaborative experience where insights can be shared and communicated directly within their consumer applications. For example, customers are increasingly spending more time in workspace collaboration tools like Slack. Recent research showed that the average Slack user has the application open 9 hours per day and spends more than 90 active minutes per day using it.

Gone are the days of leaving where you are working, going to a URL or portal, searching and loading an analysis, filtering in order to find a number, then going back to where you were working. The expectation is that analytics should be contextual and in the user's existing flow of work. This means analytics should know who you are, what your role is, and what you care about. It should be in your Slack channel or conversation, inside your opportunity records in Salesforce, embedded in your customer's portal, or displayed inside your document.

The industry is quickly responding to this need. A great example of this can be found with Tableau's new "Pulse" capability. Tableau Pulse leverages Tableau AI to reimagine the data analytics paradigm. (See Figure 16.3.) It aims to enhance the data consumer experience but ultimately it improves workflows for both IT and the business—for an IT developer or analyst, it enhances data management control, enforces data governance, and ensures data consistency by allowing for the ability to easily curate, manage, and deliver trusted KPIs.

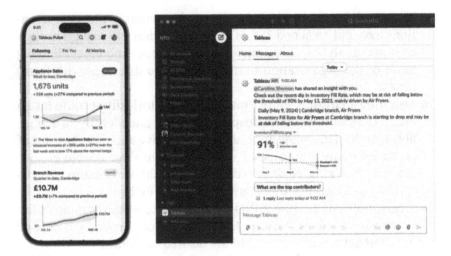

FIGURE 16.3   Tableau Pulse Enhanced by Tableau AI

At the same time, it uses AI to give data consumers proactive, personalized, contextual insights directly within the tools they use every day, whether that be in Slack, email, CRM or other third-party applications.

These "next-gen" data experiences like Tableau Pulse are producing entirely new avenues to help the non-data savvy user use data effectively. Data are becoming personalized, systems are able to automatically and proactively communicate key insights, and conversation-like end user engagement is expanding user adoption, while simultaneously eliminating a large portion of the tedious, repetitive analyst work. This will enhance the ability of the common knowledge worker to leverage accurate, relevant data as part of every important business decision and will further democratize insights across the enterprise.

SO WHAT ARE THE ORGANIZATIONAL BENEFITS?

These are just a few of the nascent capabilities that are serving as the foundation of these next generation analytics experiences. Inevitably, organizations that view analytics as a strategic priority are those that are best able to reap the benefits and differentiate from the competition. These benefits include the following:

- Improved data accessibility—As stated previously, most organizations have only reached 30% of their population with data. Through next-gen analytics, this number will drastically increase, allowing more of the organization to make grounded decisions with faster time-to-insight.
- Less time analyzing, more time acting—Historically, it could take a dozen or more questions to explore a dataset and identify an actionable insight. This made analysis time intensive and therefore out of reach for many employees. Companies want their people executing, not analyzing. Now they don't have to choose because insights can be intelligently curated and proactively delivered.
- Measurable outcomes—With greater data accessibility, more of the organization will have access to a feedback loop around whether or not their actions are leading to the desired outcomes.
- Efficiency and productivity gains—Curated insights, natural language engagement, recommended actions, and more all lead to increased employee efficiency and productivity.
- Data monetization—Most importantly, you will have the ability to drive next-gen customer experiences and develop new data products that directly contribute to your bottom line.

The future of the analytics industry will be driven by the integration of advanced AI and ML technologies, enabling real-time, predictive insights that empower faster and more accurate decision-making. With the proliferation of cloud-based solutions and the democratization of data, analytics will become more accessible to a wider range of users, fostering a data-driven culture across organizations. Additionally, enhanced accessibility to analytics in the hands of business decision-makers will further solidify their role as cornerstones of modern business strategy.

***

DATA + AI + TRUST IN THE WORKPLACE

AI Hype Versus Reality? What Does This Mean for Humans?

Andrea: *With two teens in high school field sports, I sit along the sidelines of fields pretty often. This past fall, I overheard many conversations among the seniors applying to colleges. All of these students have tinkered with ChatGPT and have seen its magic first hand.*

"College apps are terrible, maybe I'll ChatGPT my essays," one joked.

Most of these academically focused and highly aspirational kids are not truly certain of what they want to major in in college, but it seems being unsure or exploratory about the possibilities doesn't fare well in today's competitive college application process. One afternoon, I happened to overhear a conversation regarding their college application strategies.

"We have to show a demonstrated focus area for colleges but we have to find something that won't be overtaken by AI," one kid mused.

Another added, "you don't want to be a lawyer like my uncle because AI robots will replace them."

"I'm interested in environmental and civil engineering but maybe I'll apply to agriculture which could also be easier to get into. Can AI grow crops?"

"I would like to do custom woodwork," chimed in another.

Technological innovation has often threatened society's status quo. Recently, AI has led to substantial debate as to whether we should be celebrating or afraid. Early nineteenth century England saw an uprising of hand-loom weaving artisans who believed the mechanized power loom would cause mass unemployment and economic stagnation. With staunch views that innovation was destructive, these anti-technology communities, named after General Ned Ludd, became known as "Luddites." For several years, they rioted and broke into factories to destroy the power machinery in hopes of maintaining their jobs and relevance.[1]

Economists have since adopted the phrase "Luddite fallacy" to refer to the principle that while some workers are displaced, technology ultimately fuels innovation and economic growth. In the case of the automated loom, mass production of fabric led to lower prices for clothing and higher demand. Additionally, because of lower prices, consumers had higher disposable income to spend elsewhere. This led to higher interest in premium items such as hats and scarves and more demand for rail travel. Ultimately, while some workers faced structural unemployment, overall, society benefited from economic growth, and many people were able to shift into new, higher paying opportunities such as building and maintaining machines and factories.

Nevertheless, Luddite perspectives have flourished throughout history. The fact is that new technologies continually displace older ones. Ford's cars destroyed the carriage industry, ATMs changed the role of bank tellers and the rise of personal computers impacted typists and copy-machine operator jobs. For each of these examples, it's accepted that the efficiency and automation gains that led to temporary structural unemployment eventually resulted in substantial progress.

Does the Luddite fallacy hold true today when change is happening at such a head-spinning rate? Is the pace of GenAI adoption so fast that the unemployed won't have time to reorient themselves before the next wave of change? Does AI-driven displacement lead to devastating social and economic woes? Will economic value created outweigh the costs of lost employment?

And what will be the ultimate mix between AI-augmented and AI-autonomous work? Not to mention, what happens when AI is in the hands of bad actors creating deep fakes and spreading misinformation? Will AI bring utopia or Armageddon—or something in between?

Opinions vary. In 2023, Elon Musk attended the AI Safety Summit in London and was asked about AI's impact on society. He predicted:

I think we are seeing the most disruptive force in history. . .we will have for the first time something that is smarter than the smartest human. . . . There will come a point where no job is needed. . . . The AI will be able to do everything.[2]

On the other hand, Bill Gates also speaks about the implications of AI on society, but he does it with a more optimistic outlook. In a blog post, Gates said:

My work has always been rooted in a core idea: Innovation is the key to progress. . . . Innovation is the reason our lives have improved so much over the last century. From electricity and cars to medicine and planes, innovation has made the world better. Today, we are far more productive because of the IT revolution. The most successful economies are driven by innovative industries that evolve to meet the needs of a changing world.

He went on to add,

AI is about to supercharge the innovation pipeline.[3]

We lean toward Bill Gates' optimistic view, with some caution. We're optimistic that if AI is truly democratized and kept accessible at a free or reasonable price, value will be seen through overall economic growth, and the playing field will remain fair across economic classes. Most people will benefit. This assumes displaced structurally unemployed workers will be able to find new roles within a reasonable time, perhaps adjusting into new jobs that will be augmented by AI.

Access to technology should give rise to more potential entrepreneurs and businesses, who will find success in the expanding locations of opportunity. More people could take advantage of AI externalities, ultimately creating jobs and growing new markets in adjacent spaces.

VALUE WILL BE GENERATED BY GenAI

A *lot* of value. One recent McKinsey study estimated that the total economic value of GenAI "amounts to $6.1 trillion to $7.9 trillion annually."

Understanding the links in the AI value chain may give you a sense for the magnitude and timing with which you have to work to transform your company. We're all guessing at what is in our murky crystal ball—so providing some of the background may help you judge for yourself. Bear in mind that this is going to be a long, exciting journey. Figuring out what pace you want to move in light of infrastructure- and foundation-setting is important.

I (Andrea) looked at various GenAI value chains and drew largely from the work of Best Practices AI, a boutique AI consultancy firm that specializes in strategic, implementation, and responsible AI governance services. I modified their framework by flipping the order top to bottom and adding "ML and AI Operations" as an area between Applications and Foundation Models and "Services."

We are currently in phase 1 of GenAI, and I believe this phase is overhyped in practice, with the vast majority of financial value going to the infrastructure players and foundational model builders. Approximately 60% of recent venture capital funding went into the foundational model layer of the value chain. (See Figure 17.1.)

There is no doubt that in this initial phase of the GenAI revolution, the big winners are a handful of well-capitalized, now well-known, companies, their shareholders, employees, and partners. By early 2024, NVIDIA exceeded $2 trillion in market capitalization. Their revenue went from $6 billion to $22 billion in a year.[4] Starting out as a gaming-chip manufacturer, they were pioneers in breakthrough parallel processing GPUs, which are critical for AI. Their early investment in AI-related hardware and software has expanded into full stack options, essentially offering an end-to-end AI factory. Demand from big buyers like Microsoft, Google, and Meta far exceeds supply, and orders were backlogged 11 months at one point.[5] These big buyers even added GPU availability as a potential risk in their own earnings reports.

NVIDIA's infrastructure monopoly is creating a new computational center of gravity, shifting the power of hyperscalers out of their normal orbital paths. In 2024, Microsoft and OpenAI announced exploration of a $100 billion Stargate 1 project. The concept would be for Microsoft to fund supercomputing power in AI data centers in support of OpenAI's expansion.[6]

Microsoft is another early winner. It has seemingly funded, partnered with, or hired the founders from most of the hottest AI startups. Microsoft has been buying into the headlines with several investments including a $13 billion investment in OpenAI, a $3.2B investment in AI datacenters in Europe and $1 billion in Inflection, to name a few.[7] Microsoft has launched more than a dozen different Copilots (which are not easy to discern from one another) across their vast product portfolio.

Countries	Governments may want to control AI to spur their economies and protect their consumers. Support for public sector, government and regulated industries could be a significant market, economic regionalism may be more prevalent.
Industries	Industries will accelerate and capture value differently. Regulated sectors *(financial, healthcare, government)* have higher risks, higher rewards; industries with text-rich tasks, e.g., legal or knowledge management, may automate more quickly
Services	Customizations for model hubs and applications, industry-specific data sets for grounding, knowledge, change management, and execution, e.g., training, continuous learning feedback. *McKinsey, Publicis Sapient, PWC*
Applications	Customer 360: Marketing, Service, Sales, Commerce and Loyalty. Other categories include Search, Coding, RPA, Games, Image, Audio or Video Creation and industry-specialized apps. *Salesforce, Google*
ML & AI Operations	Data prep, custom model training, fine tuning, model testing, context-aware data, RAG and other tooling services. *Salesforce Data Cloud, Google, AWS, Microsoft, Databricks, Snowflake*
Foundational Models	Multimodal: text/coding, video, image, audio, tools. Microsoft, Google and Meta are competing as are highly funded ventures: *OpenAI, Anthropic, Cohere, Midjourney, Hugging Face, Mistral*
Infrastructure	Clouds: Google, Microsoft, AWS, Alibaba, Oracle
	Chips: NVIDIA, Google, Microsoft, AMD

FIGURE 17.1 The Generative AI Value Chain

Results always lag investment. A *Wall Street Journal* headline in early 2024 read: "Early Adopters of Microsoft's AI Bot Wonder if It's Worth the Money."[8] The article cited Boston Consulting Group's research that "while nearly 90% of business executives said generative AI was a top priority for their companies this year, nearly two-thirds said it would take at least two years for the technology to move beyond hype."

We don't believe these shortcomings are slowing Microsoft's pace or commitment to AI. The company's constant flow of AI announcements and activity has helped buoy Microsoft's market cap too, now over $3 trillion. During this phase 1 of GenAI, the market is demonstrating some degree of zen-like acceptance that mistakes will be made.

Phase 2 of generative AI may begin to take shape around 2025. So much money will be at stake, and it will be interesting to see if LLMs remain open source or if they will become proprietary profit-drivers. The global community generally wants LLMs to remain accessible and widely used. It's analogous to the power grid: we don't all need to be the electric company, but we need to plug into one.

The question of whether models are open, closed, or a hybrid—and by whose definition—remains very active. For example, Meta's LlaMA allowed its code, model weights, training data, evaluation, and architectural decisions to be open. However, LlaMA-2, released a bit later, while generally "open," does not have the same transparency around the source training data. Consumer attitudes or governmental regulation may soon require visibility or assurance around how the "sausage is made." If this materializes, the message again for business leaders is to prioritize data as a top strategic asset with traceability and lineage as necessary supporting features.

The negative consequences of GenAI should not be overlooked. The economic consequences for the future of work are significant for all of us. Now is the time for AI entrepreneurs, venture capitalists, legislatures, tech influencers, and people at large to make their voices heard. However, the reality is that the cost of creating an LLM and foundational model is very high and requires access to talent and resources. This suggests that most economic benefits will continue to flow to the few in the short term.

THE OTHER 99% OF HUMANS AND BUSINESSES

My capitalistic view is that businesses generally won't want to be in an egalitarian "AI democratization" phase for very long. They want to be market leaders. Natural selection of businesses suggests companies will seek profits through differentiated products and services. They want to create a competitive moat and fill it with (metaphorical) crocodiles to keep others on the far shore. They want to grow their businesses and capture margin from vendors standing in their way.

I would assert that as soon as the playing field becomes too democratized or too level, the true contenders will be those companies who assert themselves with the Customer 360 pillars of Data + AI + Trust. These contenders may not necessarily be the players with the biggest tech or talent investments, but rather those who approach the opportunity with the most operational and strategic skill.

Strategic in this context refers to skills and business acumen. These executive functions include the following:

- Setting corporate priorities with ethical use in mind
- Charting your marketplace competitive positioning
- Transforming your organizational design and culture
- Deciding on the complex tech investments and trade-offs that are picked or discarded
- Conducting your "symphony" of various AI models to win and grow your business profitably

Ironically, I believe it is those who best use *human* resources who could become the front-runners. The battle for the most talented AI-ready entrepreneurial thinkers will be a differentiator for companies.

Many have referred to the current boom fueled by generative AI as evidence of the *democratization of technology*. With its out-of-the-box accessibility, AI is now already in the hands of a large percentage of the population. Middle school students are using it to research, assist, or edit school papers; parents are using it to make trips to the grocery store more efficient.

Business executives, whether they have a bench of ML expertise on hand or not, are experimenting with base-level use cases to run their businesses more economically. The conversational nature of interacting with this technology has been *the* game-changing feature. So sure, it's democratized and usable by virtually anyone and everyone.

While we love living in a democracy, businesses are out for growth and market share. As much as this democratization levels the playing field, the onus is on companies to now find a new or unique way to differentiate. Eventually the use of generative AI will heat up, and some companies will become highly differentiated while others will become commoditized. (See Figure 17.2.)

The hype will continue through the end of this year when we will see some continued, occasional glimpses of disillusionment. Here are some approaches companies may take to GenAI—either diving straight in, dipping their toes in the water, or waiting to see how things go.

- *Diving straight in:* Company A goes after generative AI aggressively. Relying on AI too much or too quickly is riskier and could yield a big success or unfortunate failure. Risk of failure could be from employee dissatisfaction, unethical or poorly planned use leading to a bad customer response, or investing unwisely in technologies that don't deliver results. This aggressive approach may yield a bumpier ride of successes and failures along the way, but with strong executive sponsorship, Company A can still come out ahead. Using a human-at-the-helm approach alongside AI would help facilitate chances of success.

- *Dipping your toes in the water:* Company B approaches the market immediately and cautiously experiments with GenAI in a few select areas of the business. It trains all employees on AI 101 and experiments with caution—and in isolated cases, helps manage downside risks. With a mindset of continuous learning, the company gradually implements transformations needed to prime the business to use GenAI for differentiation. Employees feel part of the discovery and are accountable for the various pilot programs' success and lessons learned.

- *Wait and see:* Company C is unsure about GenAI and decides to wait and see how the market develops before doing much. Because so much transformation is required, Company C could find it difficult to catch up with those who primed their businesses today. Part of their competitive edge could quickly be undermined by competitors empowered by GenAI—in months, rather than years.

Our recommendation is to try to be Company A or Company B. The primary theme is to get AI into action today. Whether you are the

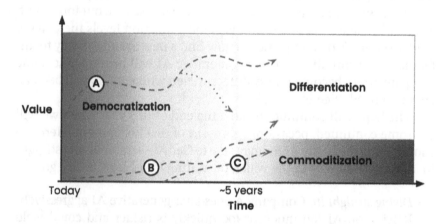

FIGURE 17.2 Creating and Capturing Value with AI

hare or the tortoise on the track, start your AI race now, even if with baby steps. In either scenario, think through the guidelines we outlined on trust and ethical use carefully.

Keeping human talent motivated and excited for massive transformation is always difficult. Some percentage of jobs will surely be affected, but for now really embrace the ways GenAI can augment human execution. Managing for change and fostering an entrepreneurial mindset are essential.

***

CHAPTER 18

Organizational Structures and Centers of Excellence

While some fear how AI will impact jobs, other see opportunity in how AI will become accessible to people broadly.

Companies are under pressure to decide how, when, and how rapidly to proceed with AI. This decision may hinge on the level of sophistication of your company when it comes to data assets, technology infrastructure, in-house talent, financial resources, and market position. In some industries, GenAI could be a game changer for those who adopt it early. Done properly some companies, even new entrants, can leapfrog existing market leaders just as companies did with e-commerce and mobile phones.

Not every company is all-in on AI—yet. According to a recent Morgan Stanley CIO survey, only 13% of companies had LLM model AI projects in production in 2023, whereas 39% expect to be in production in 2024. Interestingly, 25% had no plans to use LLMs in the near future.[1]

If you are short on technical talent, buying GenAI with a no/low code interface from the vendors you are already using to run your business is a sensible option. SaaS companies such as Salesforce offer reasonable fixed-fee subscriptions or usage-based pricing for you to get started. And the AI can be used directly in the flow of work within the applications your teams are already using.

Ultimately, our advice for business leaders is to (1) dream big, (2) execute within reach, and (3) build an adaptive culture.

> 📌 Pinned
> **Andrej Karpathy** ✅
> @karpathy
>
> The hottest new programming language is English
>
> 3:14 PM · Jan 24, 2023 · **2.8M** Views
>
> 💬 597   🔁 3,703   ❤️ 23.2K   🔖 1,652   ⬆️

FIGURE 18.1

FIRST, DREAM BIG . . .

We can only dream big if we widen the aperture of our lens. Perhaps the business you are in will be dramatically different (and better) in 3 years. Open your mind by learning as much as you can about the technology and study how others have already adopted it. Don't copy everything you see but pick and choose wisely. Businesses with a deep bench of AI engineers and data scientists may be well suited to a lot of custom work. Others want to access tools off the shelf and could work with a no/low code option like the Salesforce Einstein 1 Platform. Instead of only studying companies similar to yours, examine all types.

Participate in an AI conference from one of the companies listed in the AI Value Chain (see Chapter 17). Many companies allow virtual attendance for free. Universities like MIT are hosting events that run out of seats in days. Keep reading books from people with disparate views. Listen to podcasts from thought leaders, including the seasoned big names but also new startup chief executive officers. Make note of how you spend time in your day and where you would like to spend less. Consider how GenAI could disintermediate those areas and deliver benefits.

Execute Within Reach . . .

It is easy to get overwhelmed by concerns related to accuracy, bias, hallucinations, and privacy. Fear is overcome by incremental action: start with a few "right-sized" AI pilot projects. If you have in-house AI experts, have them oversee a group of subject-matter experts on the business problem you aim to address to ensure feasibility. If you don't have in-house expertise, consider an external AI consultant as a short-term investment. Choose a project that is not mission-critical but important enough to have a meaningful impact if successful. Bring some of these early experiments to product-grade implementations. Define measurable business outcomes that are important enough and which will generate results within two to three quarters.[2]

One of my esteemed Salesforce colleagues, Vandana Nayak, a field chief technology officer and distinguished architect, works with customers regularly to help them plan for their upcoming data and AI needs. Her workshops use the following framework. (See Figure 18.2.)

Vandana reflected on key themes from her workshops:

> Customers are all at unique and different stages of their transformation journey. What business problems are they trying to solve? It normally boils down to increasing revenue, cutting costs, or staying compliant. Rarely do projects get approved to simply explore a tool or technology—the same applies to AI. It isn't about AI for the sake of it, but where it can drive impact. So start with identifying the problems followed by figuring out the data you need to solve those problems, and finally, consider using AI to make it more efficient. Like any technology, AI is an enabler. How can it help you to be more efficient? You should be able to measure the success. You cannot improve if you cannot measure.

Implementing AI and unlocking value from your data is an ongoing journey. It is not something you do once and forget. Your models

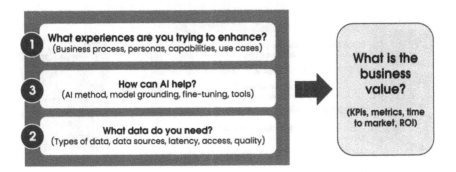

FIGURE 18.2 AI Planning Framework

continuously learn and improve. You need to experiment, stabilize, and expand to achieve real AI transformation.

By running a pilot project or conducting experiments in a sandbox, you can allow for exploration and a better understanding of GenAI, even if the project is deemed "unsuccessful." The key is gaining more organizational comfort with generative AI and learning lessons that can help you next time. (See Figure 18.3.)

In planning and executing a pilot project, we suggest the following:

- Have a strategic purpose.
- Have an executive sponsor.
- Include participation from other functional team members.
- Define metrics and milestones up front.
- Find a quick win.
- Learn from the experience (pros and cons are equally important).

Use these early learnings to pilot other experiments and boot camps.[3]

As we recommend throughout this book, design your businesses with the right combination of Data + AI + Trust that is open, extensible, and adaptable. Build AI with your (human) teams in mind and don't underestimate the importance of the user interface (UI). Without having access to a trusted UI or AI application interface in the flow of work, your teams may lose interest and even trust in the project.

Despite the changing roles employees will have in the future, putting humans at the helm of AI should be an organizational mandate.

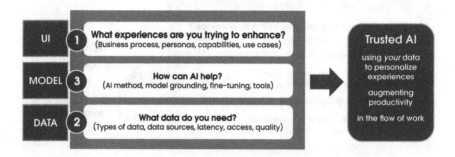

FIGURE 18.3   Create Layers of AI-Driven Experiences

BUILD AN ADAPTIVE CULTURE

Getting the cultural elements right is just as significant as deciding what LLMs to use or how to allocate your technology budget. And unfortunately, experienced practitioners tell us that almost no organization gets the culture stuff exactly right on the first try.

I asked Salesforce' practice partner Suniti Kanodia, a principal from PwC, what she observes in customers across digital transformation projects. She shared her key tips for business executives.

As she helps clients think about the "early days AI strategy," she sees some key forces emerging:

1. The need to balance the fear of being left behind and the risk of moving too quickly
2. Aligning the AI strategy with the existing digital strategy to help prevent starting from scratch
3. Thinking big but starting small with key use cases that can be scaled once they prove successful
4. Developing a productivity plan, and looking at strategically putting productivity gains to use
5. Being thoughtful of the impacts on workers, their roles and their skill-building opportunities, to include employees in building out the AI strategy
6. Teaming up with the ecosystems to rethink the value chain

LEFT-BRAINED AND RIGHT-BRAINED LEADERSHIP

Develop a plan that is strategic and methodical, yet scrappy and agile. It will take capable leadership to thrive among the new tools and complex forces ahead. In fact, being a competent leader in these circumstances requires recognition that part of success is learning quickly from failure and resetting.

The ability to introduce this novel technology—part threat, part opportunity—into the workforce with the right touch requires perspective. Ambidextrous leadership is needed. Executives will have to make partnership decisions related to technologies and companies. With GenAI, there is not a deep bench of data to draw from nor are there yet many established curricula or experts to learn from.

It seems like almost every company in high tech is announcing a GenAI product or enhancement each week. As someone who follows technology for a living, I find the narrative difficult to keep up with, and at times vendor offerings are difficult to distinguish from one another. Business leaders need to be as data driven as they can be but know when to trust their instincts too. You have to lead your teams and be optimistic and confident about a new platform, business model or organization design while also being vulnerable and willing to say you made mistakes and pivot as needed.

Managing the workforce will be complex, and you need to anticipate that employees will have mixed feelings and responses. You will need to navigate managing people to ensure they feel rewarded by integrating technology into their roles thoughtfully. You have to reward failure and reinvention during this pioneering, exploratory phase too. The stakes are high so go forward now so you can ease your way into the new world cautiously, minimizing risk and staying within ethical boundaries. There *is* room for error today, but the stakes will be higher within a year or two.

Start thinking about those areas of your business where GenAI will work successfully. Choosing the right technologies and partners to use requires the same due diligence and cultural fit required for interviewing a senior leader of your company. Choose to buy or build models that have strengths that can benefit your company and weaknesses that your business can tolerate. Have a cross-functional team meeting regularly to identify what tasks are suitable and map them on a continuum to measure, monitor, and determine how GenAI can make your employees and businesses successful. (See Figure 18.4.)

The size and breadth of companies' leadership teams will evolve to suit decision-making and focus. We're guessing that just as data and tech stacks are centralizing, it's more important to have a tightly aligned set of stakeholders. Our hypothesis is that management teams of the future will be less broad. Teams of humans will be more cross-functional. For example, sales, marketing, and go-to-market teams may be more integrated than they are today, as would product and engineering organizations. While we advocate that the next 12 to 18 months of AI experimentation bubble from the ground up, I think the subsequent phase will entail taking bigger top-down swings at capturing the opportunity.

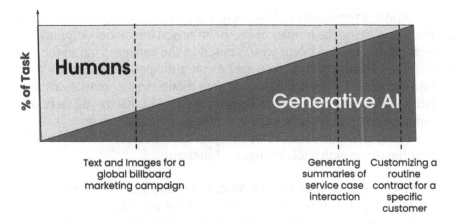

FIGURE 18.4   Human and Machine: Share of Tasks

Designing AI at too low an altitude could prevent you from realizing your full potential. For example, marketers can use AI to design optimized market segments. They can also use AI to generate subject line headers or the content of emails or push notifications. What if, harnessed properly, GenAI could be trusted to offer truly one-to-one personalized messages? Would the need for segmentation exist anymore? This is an extreme example but one that demonstrates the challenges for leaders and the scope of decision-making ahead.

NEW PARADIGM FOR HUMAN RESOURCES

Recruiting talent will change shape substantially. In fact, perhaps one of the most dramatic areas of innovation tied to AI will be how companies choose to develop, reward, organize and deploy human talent.

Human resources (HR) leaders should be investigating GenAI's possibilities in order to prepare organizations for the advantages it offers. HR may not be as focused on hiring subject-matter experts with deep experience. Rather, it will look for skilled leaders who can think like systems engineers how to make use of both human and AI resources. (See Figure 18.4.) For example, a product manager in a high tech company may no longer have to be skilled at writing a Product Requirements Document (PRD). Instead that product manager may need to be able to create a dataset with the evaluation metrics that AI can train on to produce the PRD.

And in 5 years, how will we get senior product managers to grow into the role of being the human-at-the-helm reviewing model outputs if the next group of rising talent wasn't raised in the conventional manner to become a senior product manager? As we anticipate GenAI to augment human talent, HR should have a view on model design, limitations, usability, ethical use, and more to know how GenAI impacts and facilitates human jobs, performance, execution, training, and development.

Based on a quick search, we find just a few new AI-related job titles popping up on active job listings on LinkedIn:

- Principal Specialist, GenAI, Model Training and Inference
- AI Evangelist (internal cross-organization adoption)
- Generative AI Strategist, Generative AI Innovation Center
- AI/ML Specialist, Trust and Safety

Ask yourself what you are doing to upskill your team to feel empowered by AI. GenAI will be more augmentation-oriented than automation-oriented over the next 18 to 24 months, so take advantage of that window. At any and all levels of the organization, do you have AI-forward talent in the company who are exploratory and curious? Put a premium on these people, wherever they are in the organization. You will need ambassadors for AI at all levels and across all functions to act as role models. If you can find an AI consultant to assist, consider booking him or her before it is too late.

Double-clicking into AI policy training requires entrepreneurial thinking and a continuous learning mindset. For example, Salesforce conducted a double-anonymous online survey in partnership with You-Gov in 2023. It canvassed more than 14,000 full-time employees representing companies of a variety of sizes and sectors in 14 countries. This survey showed that more than a quarter (28%) of workers are currently using GenAI at work, and more than half are using it *without* the formal approval of their employers. Of the overall survey respondents, 69% of workers said they had never completed or received training on how to use GenAI safely and ethically at work. Furthermore, 79% of respondents said they did not have clearly defined policies for using AI at works.[4] (See Figure 18.5.)

AI is not going to be a function relegated only to your IT department. Instead it will be a widespread capability spread across your entire business. Accessing ways for formal and informal training and

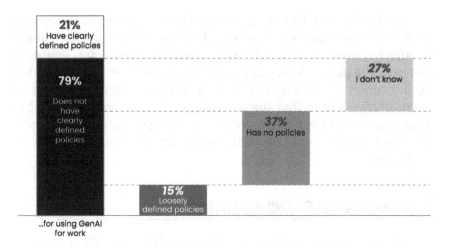

FIGURE 18.5 AI Policies in the Workplace (%)

continuous learning forums will be a key success factor for successful companies.

FOSTER A CHANGE MANAGEMENT CULTURE AND AI IQ

Related to both ambidextrous leadership and human resources is the need to instill a change management culture.

A young manager that I'm mentoring felt slighted recently from an interaction with an executive to whom he was newly aligned. The executive wanted a quick investigation into something and turned to someone else for help even though it was the young manager's responsibility. In my opinion it wasn't a big deal so I asked why he was laboring over this minimal slight so much. He responded that he had always been an exceptional student who got straight As and was not used to not being the best. I answered that I had plenty of practice dealing with such slights, starting with my commonly poor grades throughout high school. I blew off a lot of my classes and often went through the circuitous route of having to pull my grades up to a "B" or sometimes an "A" from a "C" (even a "D" once—AP Chemistry!) in the last few weeks of a semester.

My point is: don't be like my mentee. Getting GenAI right will take trial and error; we will all have to get used to making mistakes and adjusting as needed.

You need to build a change-oriented mindset in the company. You have to reward exploration and the ability and willingness to fail-fast to adjust course. From a team sports analogy standpoint, you don't just need the players who can run the 100-meter dash the fastest. You need diversity of skills on the team to take advantage of unexpected opportunities and to find the technology, cultural, and strategic balance required. Some players need to be scrappy and agile while others might bring IQ and knowledge to facilitate the most opportunistic AI outcomes.

EVOLVING OLD ROLES AND NEW ROLES

Just as the internet brought about the prevalence of a chief information officer (CIO), GenAI is bringing about the need for a chief AI officer (CAIO). CAIOs will have to figure out how to create a systemic unified data strategy. They also need the ability to determine at what altitude to create clusters of models. The number of functional leaders should correspond in some ratio to the number of models. Cross-functional teams across business, finance, and technology will work in cohorts to cultivate data for processes and subprocesses. They will also create internal policies and clarify uses and tools to ensure humans are equipped to handle data properly.

Most companies will likely have an Ethical Use or AI Policy team working closely with legal to manage risk, regulation, and compliance under the CAIO. Their guidances and guardrails will give employees clarity and ideally encourage experimentation. We should expect global governments to have additional impact on the regulatory climate for AI.

The EU AI Act of 2024 was just the beginning. While regulation is often seen as a limiting factor for business, in this context, I believe judicious regulation will help steer society toward better outcomes. Who is to blame when an autonomous AI agent causes a problematic action? AI administrators will need to be on alert when things go wrong. These teams need to have the accountability and resources to observe adversarial attacks (e.g., prompt injections) through tools such as data logs, analytics, quality, and confidence scoring to resolve issues and inject human review when necessary.[5]

Finance in the future will have to be more fluid. Priority projects may not be as easy to plan, so finance may need to design for smaller, more frequent projects on an ad hoc basis. It may be difficult to plan for budget needs on an annual budget cycle basis.

Marketing and branding will be very different. Instead of media-based marketing acquisition and search engine optimization, companies may have to attract customers through prompt-engineering acquisition. Segmentation of target marketing audiences may not exist in 5 years since AI may allow for truly one-to-one personal engagement. There will perhaps be more responsibility around communicating compliance with regulatory bodies, certainly in highly regulated spaces such as the public sector, financial services, and health care, but in other verticals as well.

HIRE CURIOSITY AND A CONTINUOUS-LEARNING MINDSET

Create collaborations in the company culture to foster a growth mindset alongside AI. Ask your teams to imagine the following:

What if anyone could quickly produce high-quality, clean code?

What if immersive training simulations vastly improve reskilling?

What if an intelligent agent could find your next role, prepare you for interviews, and negotiate your salary?

These are some of the questions the Salesforce Futures team asks in their work to help customers anticipate, imagine, and shape the future.

Curiosity has always been at the top of my list when hiring, and now it is now more critical than ever. Employees have to be willing to adapt to a new dimension of thinking. Even though conversational UI prompts are relatively easy to use, people still need to understand their technical limitations and have the judgment to be the human at the helm, accepting responsibility for the output.

Generative AI is a giant tsunami wave and its impact will likely lead to several additional waves or opportunities—some of which we can't anticipate today. Curiosity, adaptability, problem-solving, and systems thinking are the top skills to look for in your teams.

***

CHAPTER 19

Leading Through Transformation— What's Next?

The progress made in the short amount of time between ChatGPT-3.5's launch in November 2022 and GPT-4's launch in March 2023 was substantial. This improvement can be looked at two ways. One way is to see it as a threat: AI "knows" more than an average person. Another way is to think, "This technology will make me so much smarter and faster in whatever I pursue." I urge you to take the second approach.

Figure 19.1 shows that GPT-4 models have proven to be better test-takers than GPT-3.5.

WHAT'S NEXT? KEEP THE HORIZON IN SIGHT

The market shifts that GenAI will facilitate over the next 4 to 8 years will be sizable and nearly impossible to anticipate. The marginal costs to run businesses may be reduced by epic proportions—in 10 years, perhaps a 20% or 50% or even more, whether it's a reduction in the costs for computational power, customer service, building a product, or creating a movie. The competitive landscape will change radically as new entrants and existing players compete at some fraction of the current incremental cost.

At Salesforce, it is top of mind for us to not just think of transforming our own business but also how we can help our customers better serve and retain their customers through these shifts. Today the focus is to solve for the next 2 to 3 years in pragmatic terms, which primes the surface for the next generation.

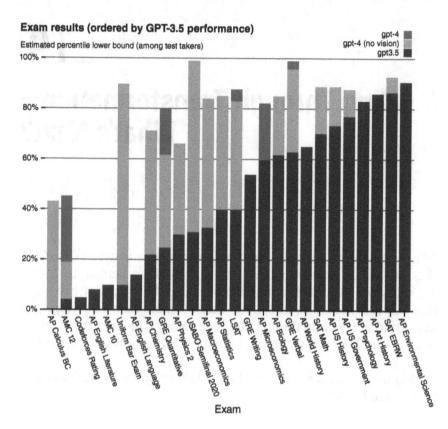

FIGURE 19.1 GPT Performance on Various Tests
Source: OpenAI

Preparing for the future of Customer 360 includes the following:

- Getting your **Data** curated and harmonized, to
- Fuel safe use of generative **AI** that improves business results, and is
- Easy to use in the flow of work in **CRM**, while being
- Rooted in **Trust**.

Most of all, leaders need to keep their brains brimming with exploratory thinking. To stay curious, keep an eye on what the prognosticators and venture capitalists are anticipating will be relevant after GenAI. Where are the investment dollars going, and what partnerships are systemic game changers? Also watch for how regulations may slow things down but provide guardrails for safer participation. Have a regular newsfeed or set of podcasts you tune into and judge different points of view for yourself. Gauge the pace of the market and anticipate what's next. Constantly plan and strategize your own game plan with offensive and defensive moves in mind.

WATCH FOR NEW REGULATIONS

Additional regulation of AI at many levels is inevitable. Elon Musk says that AI regulation "will be annoying," but that ultimately, "having a referee is a good thing, to reduce the threat to mankind."[1] The EU passed the AI Act after 3 years of deliberation. Some key themes emerged:

1. Using GenAI for unacceptable risks and deceptions will be outlawed.
2. GenAI-produced content is labeled as such.
3. Citizens can file complaints against AI systems.
4. Proprietary models must comply with model evaluations, provide algorithm documentation including parameters and weights, and respect copyright laws.[2]

Now the work for regulators to implement and enforce these laws will be substantial. In 2024, the United Nations General Assembly unanimously adopted the first global resolution on AI that encourages countries to safeguard human rights, protect personal data, and monitor AI for risks.

> "Today, all 193 members of the United Nations General Assembly have spoken in one voice, and together, chosen to govern artificial intelligence rather than let it govern us."
> —*U.S. Ambassador to the United Nations Linda Thomas-Greenfield*

In the United States, the White House issued an executive order in 2023, which detailed new standards for AI safety and security. The overarching theme is to support innovation while safeguarding its use for societal benefit. It addresses a range of factors from civil rights and privacy to consumer and employee rights. It calls for transparency and the creation of standards to ensure safety before public release.[3]

Under Section 230 of the US Communications Decency Act of 1996, internet platforms are protected from the content people post for public consumption. If person A says something defamatory on Instagram about person B, person B can sue Person A but not Instagram. Thus far, most experts don't believe the protection from Section 230 will extend to platforms that are capable of generating the content themselves. In this case, GenAI content would be considered the creator and therefore subject to harmful speech laws. Or it is plausible that generated content (as a product) could subject the GenAI process that created it to laws governing defective products. More than 500 pieces of AI-related legislation were filed in the United States as of 2024.[4]

Luddite-like responses to AI's impacts are to be expected, but the combination of world forums, government, and business leadership will minimize these disruptions. Proper regulation will help provide the foundation for innovation to thrive with due regard for ethical considerations.

GAUGE THE PACE OF THE FOURTH INDUSTRIAL REVOLUTION

AI models and training computation power have grown exponentially larger; the most powerful systems have one million times more computing capacity than a decade ago. The chief executive officer of Microsoft AI, Mustafa Suleyman, believes that AI will achieve orders-of-magnitude progress in model training size: "1000x larger in three years." But as we have seen, supply chain disruptions are already creating economic impact among the largest technology vendors vying for access to necessary chips. (See Figure 19.2.)

Even quality public data itself may be in short supply. The AI research firm Epoch estimated that large, high-quality datasets for LLMs to train on will be hard to locate by 2028. Model builders are in search of the next frontier of data sources. Some are investigating using transcriptions of YouTube videos, while others talk of training on generated data itself. Whether this yields quality synthetic data or model collapse is yet to be proven. Other innovators are focused on designing smaller models that are less data intensive and more energy efficient.[5]

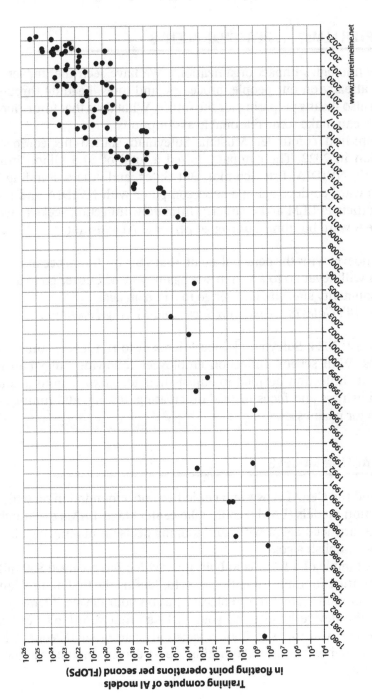

FIGURE 19.2 Training Compute of AI Models
Source: FureTimeline.net, September 10, 2023

LIFE AFTER LLMs? . . . PERSONAL AGENTS

New technologies impact organizations. We have seen the impact of GenAI already on our people, processes, and tools. Leading through change also means preparing for the future. What does that future look like? We can make some reasonable assumptions.

DeepMind cofounder Mustafa Suleyman started his company Inflection in 2022. The company raised a total of $1.5 billion from Microsoft, NVIDIA, Eric Schmidt, Bill Gates, and others. Funding is going toward co-developing a supercomputer with NVIDIA and furthering their Pi LLM and chatbot.[6] Ultimately, Inflection seeks to win the race toward building a universal personal AI assistant.

> "Whoever wins the personal agent, that's the big thing, because you will never go to a search site again, you will never go to a productivity site, you'll never go to Amazon again."
> —*Bill Gates at a Goldman Sachs and SV Angel event in 2023*

In early 2024, Suleyman joined Microsoft to run its consumer AI business. With several Inflection employees following Suleyman to Microsoft, Inflection decided to adjust their focus away from a consumer business and focus instead on creating, testing, and tuning AI systems for businesses.[7]

LARGE ACTION MODELS

LLMs and the GenAI ecosystem could become a foundation on which large action models (LAMs) could take center stage. LAMs essentially act as an artificial agent with autonomous decision-making capabilities to accomplish a goal.

An example of a LAM is Rabbit, Inc., which has received $30 million in venture funding. Rabbit's goal is to, "define the first natural language operation system that replaces apps on your device."[8] Unveiled at CES, the device handles all your tasks so that you don't need to navigate into your apps to book a vacation or to order takeout. Like Inflection, Rabbit is aimed at fulfilling the AI-driven personal assistant opportunity.

Following are some key traits of LAMs:

1. Multi-hop thinking and complex reasoning across interconnected tasks to generate actionable outputs
2. Advanced formal and functional linguistic capabilities with superior understanding of textual and external context
3. Strategic planning, pattern recognition, and self-learning that enables autonomous actions and execution[9]

MULTIMODEL, MULTIMODAL, AND MORE!

Going back to the data as fuel analogy or as today's gold, people already know curating data as a strategic asset for competitive advantage is critical. As for how they will use AI? We suspect enough large LLMs will remain open and will be good for general purpose needs. That last degree of precision will determine how widely business-critical use cases can be supported and how much humans will need to supervise the AI. Most likely, companies will have different models for different uses, and certainly some of them will be trained on their own proprietary customer data. The leading companies of the future will be those who strategically employ different types of models in a strategic, cost-effective manner and in a manner that keeps human employees engaged and at their highest productivity.

The development of multimodel capabilities is rapidly under development now and is likely to provide the foundations for next generation robotics and artificial general intelligence (AGI), which proposes the ability for machines to demonstrate problem-solving and open-ended reasoning. Following are a few examples of AGI concepts being pursued today that rival the intelligence of humans.

The rough context is that AGI will be able to manage multiple modes at once including natural language text, image, audio, and video as well as visual perception, fine motor skills, and perhaps even creativity and social and emotional engagement.

My colleagues from India came to San Francisco recently for an onsite team meeting. I asked them what they wanted to do during their visit. One answered, "I want to ride in a Waymo car." The automotive industry has proved that autonomous vehicles can be a reality. Over a few short years, leading auto manufacturers have been competing as technology and software buyers and sellers.

Paul Reitzer, founder and chief executive officer of the Marketing AI Institute, has commented on the AI multi-modal explosion he expects to see within 12 to 24 months. He refers to the ability of any data *in* (text, images, video, audio) to generate any data *out* (text, images, video, audio).[10] Now imagine this AI brain gets put in the body of a robot and how that could impact the manufacturing, construction, and logistics businesses.

Apple's Vision Pro headset is a combination of augmented reality (AR) and virtual reality (VR). Meta has an AR product called Magic Leap 2. Both have described similar applications in health care, including guiding surgical procedures, providing training for nurses, and educating patients on their health conditions with more precision.[11]

NVIDIA announced its Project GR00T as the new platform for "a general-purpose foundation model for humanoid robots."[12] Tesla's Optimus bot and fully autonomous vehicles powered by foundation models are all in this same realm of addressing physical dimensions. Another Elon Musk venture, Neuralink, recently showcased a paralyzed man with an implanted chip being able to move a computer cursor with his mind.[13] The canvas is expanding tremendously for these innovations to mature into practical applications augmenting human lives.

STATE SPACE MODELS

State space models (SSMs) are significantly smaller models, between 7 billion and 14 billion parameters, compared to an LLM like GPT-4, which has a total of 1.7 trillion parameters. SSMs are proposed to be cheaper and able to generate longer text outputs than LLMs. Zyphra, a small startup in Palo Alto, has released BlackMamba, an open-source SSM that is lightweight enough to run on a mobile device. Considered a full stack AGI company fusing the principals from neuroscience and physics, the company's end goal is to create a device and an OS that can run and self-update models regardless of internet connectivity. Zyphra devices will learn about their specific owners' preferences in real time to execute on personalized and relevant actions.[14]

CONCLUSION

Implementing a continuous loop of AI fueled by curated data across your organization offers an unprecedented amount of financial upside and perhaps personal benefit. Data guidelines must ensure secure storage, usage, and transmission that respect people's privacy in a compliant manner. AI algorithms will need to be as nondiscriminatory as we can make them and protect outcomes driven by rules such as who gets hired, who is approved for a loan, or who gets what health services. In addition, models will have to provide the tools to track lineage around generated outputs. Humans will need to be involved to monitor efficacy of tools but figuring when and how much is hard to predict. Businesses will likely have to maintain different models serving different purposes to reduce risk and build a defensible competitive moat.

The economics of one's business will change substantially with AI. I've spent a large portion of my life in professional services, and the staffing model has relied on the 1:8 partner-to-staff ratio. The economics of a consulting firm shifts dramatically with AI's ability to summarize research, conduct analysis, or document production. Perhaps clients can now own these capabilities themselves through AI tools in lieu of the significant billable hours charged. The nature of how senior talent is developed and how work is priced may be disrupted significantly. People will be less focused on mundane tasks and have opportunities in more strategic, creative, and complex roles to innovate and facilitate systems architectures.

Businesses' core value propositions must be reevaluated and tested against the backdrop of innovation and risk that AI offers. Internet accessibility and the pandemic have already spurred the rise of telehealth services to accommodate consumers' needs at any time of the day or night. Wearable sensors and IoT devices can allow for remote monitoring that can signal health issues. The pace of innovation even since the pandemic seems to have picked up significantly. It makes me believe the cure for cancer will occur in my lifetime.

It is time to get in the spirit of becoming an explorer and start looking practically at your business from the outside in to really find the opportunities. It is an era of radical transformation, and data will provide the fuel for AI to enrich, analyze, activate, and optimize insights for strategic advantage.

***

CHAPTER 20

Summing Up

*E*very company wants to deliver a great experience to its customers, but very few can do it.

So we said at the beginning of our adventure together—and we hope we've brought you a bit closer to being one of those happy few. We know it's entirely possible to deliver great end-to-end experiences if you follow the principles of Data + AI + Trust:

- *Data:* Combining and organizing customer data is a critical first step to delivering a superior Customer 360.
- *AI:* AI has unlimited potential but needs a careful approach and the right internal processes.
- *Trust:* Customers (and legislators) require the security, availability, and privacy of data, and your teams need to be able to trust automated decisions.

TO RECAP

In the **Introduction**, we started with Gucci, an Italian luxury brand that developed a way to automate service responses in a *Guccified* tone using AI. Yet we saw that most customer experiences, across the globe, fall short of this ideal—and in fact appear to be deteriorating, in part due to rising expectations. Another challenge is the obvious acceleration of the rate of change: most dramatically, ChatGPT took only 2 months to reach 100 million users, introducing the era of GenAI.

We described three levels of the AI experience (for consumers and companies): data, model, and UI. Thriving in the AI-enabled future requires a solid data foundation based on some version of a Customer Data Platform, internal (and external) models, and a useful front end. And particularly in the context of the enterprise, the entire system must be based on trust, including the safety, accuracy, completeness, timeliness, and integrity of information.

Chapter 1 brought us the high-velocity story of Formula 1, which wanted to deliver a more personalized experience to its 500 million fans around the world, most of whom will never see a race in person. Specifically, it wanted to improve the experience with its websites, communications, apps, service centers, and at the track. By capturing and organizing customer data, with consent, Formula 1 was able to show more engaging content and ads—in part, simply by recognizing which team the customer followed.

In **Chapter 2**, we suggested a framework describing how the Customer 360 provides value to the enterprise and customers. Customers benefit from more relevant and engaging experiences, more closely aligned to their preferences and needs; and they also benefit from knowing they're in a relationship based on trust. Companies derive value from higher revenues based on greater engagement and from lower costs associated with efficiency. Data as an enterprise asset also has value.

Chapter 3 presented some thought-starter ideas to unlock Customer 360 tactics—that is, specific outcomes or steps you can take to get moving. These included general areas of opportunity, like cross-selling and personalizing customer service, and a set of more specific data-triggered actions for some key industries. We also provided a consultant's perspective on managing change.

Chapter 4 introduced our "Five Forces of Customer 360" concept and matrix. It looked like this:

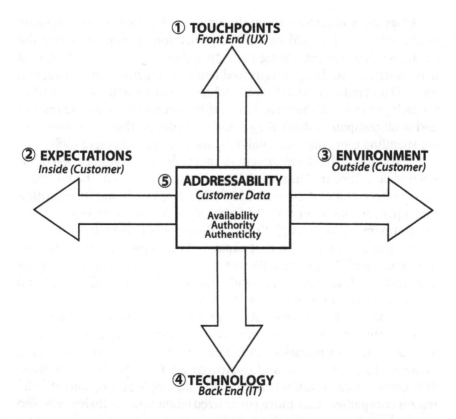

The forces are the areas of business reality with the most impact on the Customer 360. They include customers of course—specifically, their expectations—and the external environment. The other forces are related to technology, including the ways we reach customers ("touchpoints") and the systems we use. Most important, data itself is the fifth force, or rather, the addressability of customers, which is determined by data but also dimensions such as permissions, data access, and accuracy.

In **Chapter 5**, we focused more directly on the customer as a living entity. We presented a brisk tour of the state of the customer along key coordinates such as time spent with media, preferred channels, attitudes toward personalization and privacy, expressed frustrations and expectations around their experience with companies, and thoughts about AI. Finally, we unleashed our short list of 14 megatrends in customer experience right now, which included a (brief, arguably gratuitous) mention of Taylor Swift.

Chapter 6 presented some thoughts on the state of the corporate world—that is, the hard-working organizations trying to deliver the Customer 360. They're facing their own challenges, such as technical debt, complicated data, overstressed teams, competitive pressures, and more. Data volumes explode, and technical requirements ramp. Unfortunately, we saw that there is often a gap between what customers expect and what companies think they deliver. To address this gap, companies are spending more on data, analytics, and data management tools.

The story of the development of one vendor's Customer 360 offering was described in **Chapter 7**. We told the epic story of the founding of Salesforce as a cloud-based CRM ("No Software") and its evolution into a platform-as-a-service (PaaS) based on metadata. Over the years, the company opened its platform to developers and built an interoperable, flexible foundation that expanded in scope and scale with the introduction of Data Cloud. We saw how Data Cloud was built using a lake house architecture that provides the foundation for Einstein 1 and the Einstein Trust Layer supporting AI.

In **Chapter 8**, we talked about data types and sources. We traced the evolution of data storage and discussed the various different types of data in the organization: demographic, transactional, behavioral, firmographic, structured, and unstructured. Data gravity is the force that causes data to attract more data and applications, and it's the reason companies with more (organized) data tend to thrive. We also touched on the vector database and its growing importance in preparing unstructured data for use by AI systems.

Chapter 9 was devoted to customer data in the enterprise today. Both overlap and questions about the distinct roles of various data-handling systems such as CDPs, Data warehouses, MDM, and so on persist. This chapter described the differences and how they work together. CDP is a natural evolution of CRM adapted to B2C scale. MDM is a rigorous set of tools and processes to describe and manage data, but it isn't data itself. Data warehouses are still common, and data lakes arose to handle massive cloud storage with no ETL requirements. Later, modern data warehouses such as Snowflake were built from the ground up on the cloud and support zero-copy data sharing. It's common and not discouraged for an enterprise to have all these systems and more working in tandem.

The hot topics of "composability" and zero-copy were discussed in **Chapter 10**. Composability is an architectural concept that describes a system that is made up of discrete Lego-like blocks that function together but can be separated. Since it is not a product but a design choice, composability can be inherent in products such as full-featured CDPs, which can be both packaged and partly composable. The related concept of zero-copy described a versatile method of sharing data among systems without moving or transforming it.

Chapter 11 moved on to the idea of "real time" and what it really means. Commonly misunderstood to imply (1) that all data in a data management system can (or should) be available instantly and (2) the Customer 360 won't work unless total and instant access pertains. We see that there is a trade-off among cost, complexity, and real-time elements: it's not feasible for all data to be "in memory" at all times. Luckily, it's also not necessary: many Customer 360 use cases don't require sub-millisecond responses. The key is to differentiate those that do from those that don't.

In **Chapter 12**, we address the all-important topic of AI in action today. Some of the factors leading to the current AI revolution were the scale of the availability of public data sources, an increase in computational power, the maturing of AI technologies, and the ease of use of applications such as ChatGPT. We ask whether GenAI will impact the business right away and answer yes, but the biggest impact is in the future. Meanwhile, we recommend grounding prompts in first-party data and focusing on specific short-term use cases.

Chapter 13 was about trust: How can we trust AI? New AI models are not an unmixed blessing, and we describe some of their inherent risks. These risks include bias, toxicity, complexity, lack of explainability and reliability, and excessive energy use. We argue that these risks are real, but that the biggest risk is ignoring AI. We recommend a trust framework embedded in your AI application processes to filter out bias and toxicity and to enforce privacy and prevent data leakage. Ultimately, we argue that having a "human at the helm" is the safest approach for your Customer 360.

We talked about data collaboration in **Chapter 14**. The past few years in particular have seen a rising emphasis on first-party data—in part due to browser cookie deprecation, but also privacy legislation, consumer expectations for personalization, improved data collection and analytical techniques, and now the AI training imperative. Many enterprises are exploring data collaboration to expand and enrich their data. Technologies such as data clean rooms and retail media networks support collaboration, often while preserving privacy, and they work in conjunction with CDPs.

Chapter 15 was about privacy, compliance, and consent. We described the four key players in privacy discussions: web browsers, operating systems, and standards bodies; government regulators; consumers; and companies. Policies enacted by the two major browser and operating system manufacturers (Google and Apple) have had a major impact on customer experience professionals. Likewise, legislation such as Europe's GDPR forced companies to change their tactics. We describe four ways to build customer trust in an environment of rising paranoia.

In **Chapter 16,** we touched on the future of analytics in the enterprise. We already see the adoption of no-code and low-code analytical tools and, more recently, the use of natural-language prompts to query data. In the future, advanced analytics will be available to many more people across the enterprise, as innovations in AI make tools much easier to use.

Chapter 17 turned to the human side of the AI shakeup. We looked at the GenAI value chain and saw that most investment in the current phase is going to foundational and infrastructure companies. This means that most of the short-term benefit will accrue to a relative handful of high-profile, well-funded companies such as Microsoft, NVIDIA, and OpenAI. Nevertheless, we recommend engaging with AI right away, recognizing that your teams will have a lot to learn.

Chapter 18 talked about organizational structures and centers of excellence. We recommended the approach of (1) dreaming big, (2) executing within reach, and (3) building an adaptive culture. Organizations are all at different stages in their journey of transformation. Starting with a no-limits mindset, it's important to ground initial experiments in specific, contained business cases. Meanwhile, any AI strategy has to align with the existing digital strategy to prevent rework. And the impact on employees should be carefully considered.

Finally, in **Chapter 19** we looked into the future. Preparing for the future of Customer 360 begins with getting data curated and harmonized to fuel safe use of AI that improves business results. Your technology should be incorporated into the flow of work in your CRM, while also being rooted in trust. As new regulations and even newer technologies—including autonomous agents—appear, we recommend considering the short- and long-term impacts on the economics of the business, the nature of work, team dynamics, and even work-life balance. All will be affected.

In the end, we'd like to return to our original formula: Data + AI + Trust. Therein lies the key to the Customer 360 and the secret to unleashing a new dimension of experience for your customers. Wherever you are in your journey, we know there's a platform to support you. Accomplished with respect and a spirit of adventure, the Customer 360 really can change everything.

***

Notes

INTRODUCTION

1. W. P. Carey School of Business at Arizona State University. "Historic National Customer Rage Survey: Record Level of Product and Service Problems Incite Surly Customers to Yell More and Seek Revenge for Their Hassles." *PR Newswire* (March 7, 2023).

CHAPTER 2

1. Laney, D. B. *Infonomics*. Routledge, 2017.

CHAPTER 4

1. Porter, Michael E. "How Competitive Forces Shape Strategy." *Harvard Business Review* (March–April 1979).
2. McKinsey Marketer Pulse Survey (2023, $n = 100$).

CHAPTER 5

1. Turner, M. *4 marketing principles that will keep customers coming back*. Salesforce (September 5, 2023). https://www.salesforce.com/blog/connected-customer-experience/.
2. Originally appeared: Kihn, M. "14 Mega-Trends in marketing right now." *Forbes* (March 14, 2024). https://www.forbes.com/sites/forbescommunicationscouncil/2024/03/12/14-mega-trends-in-marketing-right-now/.
3. Graham, M. "Average CMO tenure holds steady at lowest level in decade." *Wall Street Journal* (May 5, 2022). https://www.wsj.com/articles/average-cmo-tenure-holds-steady-at-lowest-level-in-decade-11651744800.

CHAPTER 6

1. Digital Transformation Institute. The disconnected customer: What digital customer experience leaders teach us about reconnecting with customers. https://www.capgemini.com/wp-content/uploads/2017/07/the_discon nected_customer-what_digital_customer_experience_leaders_teach_us_ about_reconnecting_with_customers.pdf.
2. "Managing marketing technology, growth, and sustainability." *The CMO Survey*, 32nd ed., 2024. https://cmosurvey.org/wp-content/uploads/2024/04/ The_CMO_Survey-Topline_Report-Spring_2024.pdf.
3. Zylo. Zylo's 2024 SAAS management index: Say no to the status quo. (February 27, 2024). https://zylo.com/2024-saas-management-index/.
4. IAB. State of data 2024: How the digital ad industry is adapting to the privacy-by-design ecosystem (March 14, 2024). https://www.iab.com/ insights/2024-state-of-data-report/.

CHAPTER 8

1. Deloitte. Data: A small four-letter word which has grown exponentially to such a big value. https://www2.deloitte.com/cy/en/pages/technology/arti cles/data-grown-big-value.html.
2. Castagna, R. Structured vs. unstructured data: The key differences. Tech-Target, 2021. https://www.techtarget.com/whatis/feature/Structured-vs-unstructured-data-The-key-differences.
3. Weiss, K. "US Tech North America: 4Q23 CIO survey—AI rises to the top of the CIO's priority list." *Morgan Stanley Research* (2024).

CHAPTER 9

1. Bugajski, J. *Data Integration: Fantasies and Facts.* Burton Group, 2008.
2. Raab, D. I've Discovered a New Class of System: The Customer Data Platform. Causata Is an Example. https://customerexperiencematrix.blogspot .com/2013/04/ive-discovered-new-class-of-system.html.
3. Raab, D. I've Discovered a New Class Of System: The Customer Data Platform. Causata Is an Example. https://customerexperiencematrix. blogspot.com/2013/04/ive-discovered-new-class-of-system.html.
4. Winterberry Group. Demystifying the Data Layer: The Transformation of Marketing Data Infrastructure. https://winterberrygroup.com/demystifying-the-data-layer-feb2024.

5. Brinker, S. "Can Martech Data Be Unified, Federated, and Siloed All at the Same Time? Yes, and Each Serves a Purpose." *Chief Marketing Technologist* (March 4, 2024). https://chiefmartec.com/2024/03/can-martech-data-be-unified-federated-and-siloed-all-at-the-same-time-yes-and-each-serves-a-purpose/.

CHAPTER 10

1. Wallace, D. CDP market trends in 2024. IDC, 2024. https://www.idc.com/getdoc.jsp?containerId=US51933224.
2. Rydning, J. Worldwide IDC Global DataSphere Forecast, 2023–2027: It's a distributed, diverse, and dynamic (3D) DataSphere. IDC Research, 2023. https://www.idc.com/getdoc.jsp?containerId=US50554523.

CHAPTER 12

1. Queensland Brain Institute. History of Artificial Intelligence. University of Queensland, Australia. https://qbi.uq.edu.au/brain/intelligent-machines/history-artificial-intelligence.
2. Queensland Brain Institute. History of Artificial Intelligence. University of Queensland, Australia. https://qbi.uq.edu.au/brain/intelligent-machines/history-artificial-intelligence.
3. Eubanks, B. AI concepts: What Is Moravec's Paradox and Why Should You Care? Lighthouse Research and Advisory, 2018. https://lhra.io/blog/ai-concepts-moravecs-paradox-care/.
4. AI Frontiers. "Andrew Ng at AI Frontiers Conference 2017: AI Is the New Electricity." YouTube, November 13, 2017. https://www.youtube.com/watch?v=JsGPh-HOqjY&t=2739s.
5. Staff. Deep Learning vs. Machine Learning: A Beginner's Guide. Coursera, 2024. https://www.coursera.org/articles/ai-vs-deep-learning-vs-machine-learning-beginners-guide.
6. *Toward a Hybrid AI Platform.* Salesforce Research & Insights team, 2024.
7. Cohen, J. and Lee, G. The Generative World Order: AI, Geopolitics, and Power. Goldman Sachs, 2023. https://www.goldmansachs.com/intelligence/pages/the-generative-world-order-ai-geopolitics-and-power.html#:~:text=The%20most%20profound%20impact%20of,GDP%20by%20nearly%20%247%20trillion.
8. The State of AI in 2023: Generative AI's Breakout Year. McKinsey & Company, 2023. https://www.mckinsey.com/capabilities/quantumblack/our-insights/the-state-of-ai-in-2023-generative-ais-breakout-year.

9. The State of AI in 2023: Generative AI's Breakout Year. McKinsey & Company, 2023. https://www.mckinsey.com/capabilities/quantumblack/our-insights/the-state-of-ai-in-2023-generative-ais-breakout-year.

10. The State of AI in 2023: Generative AI's Breakout Year. McKinsey & Company, 2023. https://www.mckinsey.com/capabilities/quantumblack/our-insights/the-state-of-ai-in-2023-generative-ais-breakout-year.

11. De Smet, A., S. Durth, B. Hancock, M. Mugayar-Baldocchi, and A. Reich, "The Human Side of Generative AI: Creating a Path to Productivity." *McKinsey Quarterly* (March 18, 2024). https://www.mckinsey.com/capabilities/people-and-organizational-performance/our-insights/the-human-side-of-generative-ai-creating-a-path-to-productivity?stcr=8D2D032EFBCD4095A2CC9938AA5F74C7&cid=other-eml-alt-mip-mck&hlkid=92823fe4a953474595f43da8d003a0eb&hctky=15450690&hdpid=746f6093-9461-49fe-8060-faf811e5e762.

12. Davis, D. How L'Oréal Uses AI to Stay Ahead of Its Competition. Digital Commerce 360, 2022. https://www.digitalcommerce360.com/2022/02/24/how-loreal-uses-ai-to-stay-ahead-of-its-competition/.

13. Doolan, K. How L'Oréal Uses AI to Stay Ahead of Its Competition. Cosmetics Design Europe, 2024. https://www.cosmeticsdesign-europe.com/Article/2024/03/18/L-Oreal-CMO-on-how-to-market-a-beauty-brand-in-2024.

14. Dubey, A. Augmented marketing in beauty with generative AI. Nvidia GTC Session, 2024. https://resources.nvidia.com/en-us-generative-ai-for-retail/gtc24-s62335.

15. Lakhani, K. "AI Won't Replace Humans—But Humans With AI Will Replace Humans Without AI." *Harvard Business Review* (August 4, 2023). https://hbr.org/2023/08/ai-wont-replace-humans-but-humans-with-ai-will-replace-humans-without-ai.

CHAPTER 13

1. World Economic Forum. "Future of Jobs Report 2023." 2023. https://www3.weforum.org/docs/WEF_Future_of_Jobs_2023.pdf.

2. OpenAI. "Sora: Creating Video from Text." Openai.com. OpenAI. February 15, 2024. https://openai.com/sora

3. Clark, E. "Tyler Perry Warns of AI Threat after Sora Debut Halts an $800 Million Studio Expansion." *Forbes* (March 11, 2024). https://www.forbes.com/sites/elijahclark/2024/02/23/tyler-perry-warns-of-ai-threat-to-jobs-after-viewing-openai-sora/?sh=59353bca7071.

4. Katz, S. "How can we make AI less biased against disabled people." Fast Company (March 11, 2024). https://www.fastcompany.com/91054056/how-we-can-make-ai-less-biased-against-disabled-people.

5. Power-Hungry AI: Researchers Evaluate Energy Consumption across Models. Computer Science and Engineering, University of Michigan (August 14, 2023). https://cse.engin.umich.edu/stories/power-hungry-ai-researchers-evaluate-energy-consumption-across-models.

6. State of the Connected Customer. 6th ed. Salesforce, 2023. https://www.salesforce.com/content/dam/web/en_us/www/documents/research/State-of-the-Connected-Customer.pdf.

7. Baxter, K., and Y. Schlesinger. "Managing the Risks of Generative AI." *Harvard Business Review* (June 6, 2023). https://hbr.org/2023/06/managing-the-risks-of-generative-ai.

8. Lakhani, K. "AI Won't Replace Humans—but Humans with AI Will Replace Humans without AI." *Harvard Business Review* (August 4, 2023). https://hbr.org/2023/08/ai-wont-replace-humans-but-humans-with-ai-will-replace-humans-without-ai.

9. Artificial Intelligence Is Helping Deliver Cancer Outcomes Better than the National Average. Moffitt Cancer Center, 2024. https://www.moffitt.org/for-healthcare-professionals/clinical-perspectives/clinical-perspectives-story-archive/artificial-intelligence-is-helping-deliver-cancer-outcomes-better-than-the-national-average/.

10. Li, O. "Artificial Intelligence Is the New Electricity—Andrew Ng." *Medium* (April 28, 2017). https://medium.com/syncedreview/artificial-intelligence-is-the-new-electricity-andrew-ng-cc132ea6264.

11. Mosaic Research Team. Introducing DBRX: A New State-of-The-Art Open LLM. Databricks, 2024. https://www.databricks.com/blog/introducing-dbrx-new-state-art-open-llm.

12. OpenAI. "What Is ChatGPT?" 2023. https://help.openai.com/en/articles/6783457-what-is-chatgpt.

13. Grynbaum, M. M., and R. Mac. "The Times Sues OpenAI and Microsoft over A.I. Use of Copyrighted Work." *New York Times* (December 27, 2023). https://www.nytimes.com/2023/12/27/business/media/new-york-times-open-ai-microsoft-lawsuit.html; Stempel, J. "Nvidia Is Sued by Authors over AI Use of Copyrighted Works." *Reuters* (March 11, 2024). https://www.reuters.com/technology/nvidia-is-sued-by-authors-over-ai-use-copyrighted-works-2024-03-10/#:~:text=March%2010%20(Reuters)%20%2D%20Nvidia,opens%20new%20tab%20AI%20platform.

14. Kahn, J. "It's about Better Data, Not Big Data, Deep Learning Pioneer Ng Says." *Fortune* (June 21, 2022). https://fortune.com/2022/06/21/andrew-ng-data-centric-ai/.

CHAPTER 14

1. Petro, G. "As Third-Party Cookies Fade, Brands Get Personal." *Forbes* (February 10, 2023). https://www.forbes.com/sites/gregpetro/2023/02/10/as-third-party-cookies-fade-brands-get-personal/?sh=2c8593677577.
2. Tracy, R. "3 Future-Proofing Strategies for Google's Third-Party Cookie Crackdown." *MarTech* (March 1, 2024). https://martech.org/3-future-proofing-strategies-for-googles-third-party-cookie-crackdown/.
3. Mcclain, C., M. Faverio, M. Anderson, and E. Park. "1. Views of Data Privacy Risks, Personal Data and Digital Privacy Laws." *Pew Research Center: Internet, Science & Tech* (October 18, 2023). https://www.pewresearch.org/internet/2023/10/18/views-of-data-privacy-risks-personal-data-and-digital-privacy-laws/.
4. Adams, P. "Data Marketing Spend Tops $29B in US as Cookie Deadline Looms." *Marketing Dive* (January 24, 2022). https://www.marketingdive.com/news/data-marketing-spend-tops-29b-in-us-as-cookie-deadline-looms/617539/.
5. Hercher, J. "After a Two-Year Quiet Phase, Amazon's Data Clean Room Service Enters the Market." *AdExchanger* (October 26, 2021). https://www.adexchanger.com/online-advertising/after-a-two-year-quiet-phase-amazons-data-clean-room-service-enters-the-market/.
6. Perloff, C. "Disney's Clean Room Brand Activations Grew 573% in 2023." *Adweek* (January 10, 2024). https://www.adweek.com/convergent-tv/disneys-clean-room-brand-activations-grew-573-in-2023/.
7. Wood, C. "Pinterest Announces Clean Room Partnership with LiveRamp." *MarTech* (January 6, 2023). https://martech.org/pinterest-announces-clean-room-partnership-with-liveramp/.
8. 2024 Connectivity Benchmark Report. MuleSoft, 2024. https://www.mulesoft.com/lp/reports/connectivity-benchmark.

CHAPTER 15

1. Rodenhausen, D., L. Wiener, K. Rogers, and M. Katerman. *Consumers Want Privacy. Marketers Can Deliver*. BCG Global, 2023.
2. Browne, R. "Europe and the US Finally Agree a Landmark Data-Sharing Pact—And It's Already Under Threat." *CNBC* (July 12, 2023).
3. State of the Connected Customer. 6th ed. Salesforce, 2023.
4. Atske, S., and S. Atske. Americans and Privacy: Concerned, Confused and Feeling Lack of Control Over Their Personal Information. Pew Research Center, 2024.

5. Fisher, L. "Digital Marketing in Today's Privacy-Conscious World." *Emarketer* (July 9, 2019).

CHAPTER 16

1. Arthur, C. "Tech Giants May Be Huge, but Nothing Matches Big Data." *Guardian* (December 1, 2017). https://www.theguardian.com/technology/2013/aug/23/tech-giants-data.
2. Forecast: Enterprise Application Software, Worldwide, 2021-2027, 2Q23 Update. Gartner Research, 2023.

CHAPTER 17

1. Thomas, R. J. "The Rise of Large Action Models, LAMs: How AI Can Understand and Execute Human Intentions?" *Medium* (January 16, 2024). https://medium.com/version-1/the-rise-of-large-action-models-lams-how-ai-can-understand-and-execute-human-intentions-f59c8e78bc09.
2. Thomas, R. J. "The Rise of Large Action Models, LAMs: How AI Can Understand and Execute Human Intentions?" *Medium* (January 16, 2024). https://medium.com/version-1/the-rise-of-large-action-models-lams-how-ai-can-understand-and-execute-human-intentions-f59c8e78bc09.
3. Thomas, R. J. "The Rise of Large Action Models, LAMs: How AI Can Understand and Execute Human Intentions?" *Medium* (January 16, 2024). https://medium.com/version-1/the-rise-of-large-action-models-lams-how-ai-can-understand-and-execute-human-intentions-f59c8e78bc09.
4. "Nvidia's Market Cap Finished the Day above $2 Trillion." *Wall Street Journal* (March 1, 2024). https://www.wsj.com/livecoverage/stock-market-today-dow-jones-03-01-2024/card/nvidia-s-market-cap-is-poised-to-finish-the-day-above-2-trillion-V9vUOlZqo0SAVrLXIN3B.
5. Shilov, A. "Wait Times for Nvidia's AI GPUs Ease to Three to Four Months, Suggesting Peak in Near-Term Growth—the Wait List for an H100 Was Previously Eleven Months: UBS." *Tom's Hardware* (February 16, 2024). https://www.tomshardware.com/tech-industry/artificial-intelligence/wait-times-for-nvidias-ai-gpus-eases-to-three-to-four-months-suggesting-peak-in-near-term-growth-the-wait-list-for-an-h100-was-previously-eleven-months-ubs.
6. Gardizy, A. and A. Efrati. "Microsoft and OpenAI Plost $100 Billion Stargate AI Supercomputer." *Information* (March 20, 2024). https://www.theinformation.com/articles/microsoft-and-openai-plot-100-billion-stargate-ai-supercomputer?rc=uygdtd.

7. Smith, B. "Our Investment in AI Infrastructure, Skills and Security to Boost the UK's AI Potential." *Microsoft on the Issues* (November 30, 2023). https://blogs.microsoft.com/on-the-issues/2023/11/30/uk-ai-skilling-security-datacenters-investment/.

8. Dotan, T. "Early Adopters of Microsoft's AI Bot Wonder If It's Worth the Money." *Wall Street Journal* (February 13, 2024). https://www.wsj.com/tech/ai/early-adopters-of-microsofts-ai-bot-wonder-if-its-worth-the-money-2e74e3a2.

CHAPTER 18

1. "4Q23 CIO Survey—AI Rises to the Top of CIO's Priority List." *Morgan Stanley Research* (January 22, 2024).

2. Lakhani, K. "AI Won't Replace Humans—but Humans with AI Will Replace Humans without AI." *Harvard Business Review* (August 4, 2023). https://hbr.org/2023/08/ai-wont-replace-humans-but-humans-with-ai-will-replace-humans-without-ai.

3. Naleszkiewicz, K. "Developing a Strategy for Integrating Generative AI." *Medium* (February 28, 2024). https://generativeai.pub/developing-a-strategy-for-integrating-generative-ai-53d9457fc2a0.

4. More than Half of Generative AI Adopters Use Unapproved Tools at Work. Salesforce, 2023. https://www.salesforce.com/news/stories/ai-at-work-research/.

5. Baxter, K., and Y. Schlesinger. "How Companies Can Build Trustworthy AI Assistants." *Harvard Business Review* (November 27, 2023). https://hbr.org/2023/11/how-companies-can-build-trustworthy-ai-assistants.

CHAPTER 19

1. Seal, T. and Bloomberg. "Elon Musk Says AI Regulation 'Will Be Annoying' But, Ultimately, 'Having a Referee Is a Good Thing' to Reduce the Threat to Mankind." *Fortune* (November 2, 2022). https://fortune.com/2023/11/02/elon-musk-ai-regulations-uk-prime-minister-sunak-ai-safety-summit/.

2. Heikkila, M. "The AI Act Is Done. Here's What Will (and Won't) Change." *MIT Technology Review* (March 19, 2024). https://www.technologyreview.com/2024/03/19/1089919/the-ai-act-is-done-heres-what-will-and-wont-change/.

3. Fact Sheet: President Biden Issues Executive Order on Safe, Secure, and Trustworthy Artificial Intelligence. The White House (October 30, 2023). https://www.whitehouse.gov/briefing-room/statements-releases/2023/10/30/

fact-sheet-president-biden-issues-executive-order-on-safe-secure-and-trustworthy-artificial-intelligence/.

4. Bousquette, I. "AI Is Moving Faster than Attempts to Regulate It. Here's How Companies Are Coping." *Wall Street Journal* (March 27, 2024). https://www.wsj.com/articles/ai-is-moving-faster-than-attempts-to-regulate-it-heres-how-companies-are-coping-7cfd7104?mod=Searchresults_pos8&page=1.

5. Seetharaman, D. "For Data-Guzzling AI Companies, the Internet Is Too Small." *Wall Street Journal* (April 1, 2024). https://www.wsj.com/tech/ai/ai-training-data-synthetic-openai-anthropic-9230f8d8.

6. Heaven, W. D. "DeepMind's Cofounder: Generative AI Is Just a Phase. What's Next Is Interactive AI." *MIT Technology Review* (September 15, 2023). https://www.technologyreview.com/2023/09/15/1079624/deepmind-inflection-generative-ai-whats-next-mustafa-suleyman/.

7. Weise, K., and C. Metz. "Microsoft Hires DeepMind Co-Founder to Run Consumer A.I." *New York Times* (March 19, 2024). https://www.nytimes.com/2024/03/19/technology/mustafa-suleyman-google-gemini.html.

8. PeacemongerNetworkdotcom. "Large Action Model (LAM) Explained." YouTube (January 10, 2024). https://youtu.be/o2lKl7RMb3Y.

9. SuperAGI. "Difference between LLMs vs LAMs." LinkedIn. Accessed May 22, 2024. https://www.linkedin.com/posts/superagi_large-language-models-llms-vs-large-agentic-activity-7130503954433527809-8L0y?

10. Roetzer, P., and M. Kaput. "Google I/O, GPT-4o, and Ilya Sutskever's Surprise Departure from OpenAI." Artificial Intelligence Podcast. Accessed May 22, 2024. https://www.marketingaiinstitute.com/podcast-showcase

11. Mukherjee, S. "Apple Wants Vision Pro to Be a Medical Hub. Here's How Some Health Organizations Are Already Using It." *Fast Company* (March 21, 2024). https://www.fastcompany.com/91055214/apple-vision-pro-medical-hub-health-organizations-already-using-it; Magic Leap 2 (website). https://www.magicleap.com/magic-leap-2?

12. Heater, B. "Nvidia Enlists Humanoid Robotics' Biggest Names for New AI Platform, GR00T." *TechCrunch* (March 18, 2024) .https://techcrunch.com/2024/03/18/nvidia-enlists-humanoid-robotics-biggest-names-for-new-ai-platform-gr00t/.

13. Winkler, R., and A. Corse. "Elon Musk's Neuralink Shows First Patient Using Its Brain Implant." *Wall Street Journal* (March 20, 2024). https://www.wsj.com/tech/neuralink-shows-first-patient-using-its-brain-implant-device-67a8b03a.

14. Palazzolo, S. "What to Make of OpenAI's New Board; The Startup Tackling Karpathy's Vision. *Information* (March 11, 2024). https://www.theinformation.com/articles/what-to-make-of-openais-new-board-the-startup-tackling-karpathys-vision?rc=uygdtd.

Acknowledgments

We would like to thank the ohana at Salesforce for making this book possible: John Taschek for being a fearless leader; Jay Wilder, Bobby Jania, Ryan Stryznaka, Steve Hammond, and Patrick Stokes for advice and support; and the fantastic Data Cloud product and engineering team, including Rahul Auradkar, Muralidhar Krishnaprasad (aka "MK2"), Gabrielle Tao, Bradley Wright, Gabe Joynt, Jason Ellman, Vandana Gangwar, and Brynna Evans.

We are truly grateful for the stewardship of Kathy Baxter, principal architect of the Ethical AI Practice at Salesforce, whose pioneering work and collaboration on responsible AI helped us with this book, but more broadly, helps Salesforce deliver on our number one value, trust. We received much needed advice and thought leadership from the Corporate Strategy's Analytics team, Mitchell Grewer and Will Pitzler, and from Research & Insights Principal Researcher Britta Fiore-Gartland. Field CTO and Distinguished Architect Vandana Nayak and Principal SE of the Data Cloud Thomas Boersma provided customer insights and real-world experiences to keep us honest about the opportunities and challenges ahead. Also invaluable were the perspectives shared by our partners, Publicis Sapient, senior director of Salesforce Solutions Consulting; Don Dew, PwC Principal; Suniti Kanodia; and independent AI, data, and marketing consultant, Stephanie Foster.

And of course, heartfelt gratitude to our partners at Wiley: Jeanenne Ray, Michelle Hacker, Casper Barbour, Gabriela Mancuso; our hardworking copyeditor, Sheryl Nelson of PermaFrost; and our artist, Senarath D.

About the Authors

Martin Kihn is senior vice president of market strategy for Salesforce, where he provides market guidance and product insights for the world's #1 Marketing Cloud. Before joining Salesforce, he led the data-driven marketing practice as research vice president at Gartner, focusing on marketing data integration and analytics. After earning his MBA from Columbia Business School, he worked for a time as a management consultant—an experience described in his book, *House of Lies*, which was the basis for a Showtime series. He is the author of two other memoirs, coauthor with Chris O'Hara of *Customer Data Platforms: Use People Data to Power Marketing Transformation* (Wiley), and his work has appeared in *Forbes*, *Fast Company*, the *New York Times*, *New York*, *AdExchanger*, and many other publications.

Andrea Chen Lin, a vice president of corporate strategy at Salesforce, manages the team driving successful growth and customer success using next generation technologies including data, AI, analytics, automation, integration, and digital (marketing and commerce). Prior to Salesforce, Andrea was the founder and CEO of Pareto Strategy, Inc. a boutique advisory firm that served clients based in North America and Asia Pacific, from venture funded startups to Global 1000 companies across enterprise software, consumer products, media, technology, and health and wellness markets for more than 20 years. Her work included serving as interim CEO or general manager of several companies driving new product launch, international market expansion, business planning, fundraising to exit, and operational execution. Andrea received her MBA from Harvard and her bachelor's degree from the University of Pennsylvania. Andrea lives in the Bay Area with her husband, two teenagers, and two dogs. She also enjoys serving on the board of directors of USA Lacrosse.

Index

Page numbers followed by *f* refer to figures.